Early praise for *Build Reactive Websites with RxJS*

This book provides a programmatic path that builds a constructive understanding of RxJS and its many operators for both the novice and experienced JavaScript developer.

➤ **Nathan Brenner**
   Software Engineer, Mainz Brady Group

This book provides practical approaches to understand the basics of RxJS observables and the power of operators, as well as showing how to apply them to build actual applications.

➤ **OJ Kwon**
   RxJS core team member

This book makes learning RxJS from scratch easy and fun. The real-world exercises interactively demonstrate each new concept, building on the previous ones.

➤ **Chris Thielen**
   Maintainer, UI-Router

Build Reactive Websites with RxJS

Master Observables and Wrangle Events

Randall Koutnik

The Pragmatic Bookshelf

Raleigh, North Carolina

Many of the designations used by manufacturers and sellers to distinguish their products are claimed as trademarks. Where those designations appear in this book, and The Pragmatic Programmers, LLC was aware of a trademark claim, the designations have been printed in initial capital letters or in all capitals. The Pragmatic Starter Kit, The Pragmatic Programmer, Pragmatic Programming, Pragmatic Bookshelf, PragProg and the linking *g* device are trademarks of The Pragmatic Programmers, LLC.

Every precaution was taken in the preparation of this book. However, the publisher assumes no responsibility for errors or omissions, or for damages that may result from the use of information (including program listings) contained herein.

Our Pragmatic books, screencasts, and audio books can help you and your team create better software and have more fun. Visit us at *https://pragprog.com*.

The team that produced this book includes:

Publisher: Andy Hunt
VP of Operations: Janet Furlow
Managing Editor: Susan Conant
Development Editor: Brian MacDonald
Copy Editor: Paula Robertson
Indexing: Potomac Indexing, LLC
Layout: Gilson Graphics

For sales, volume licensing, and support, please contact *support@pragprog.com*.

For international rights, please contact *rights@pragprog.com*.

ISBN-13: 978-1-68050-295-4
Book version: P1.0—December 2018

Contents

Introduction

Hello! If you've picked up this book, you've probably spent some time developing websites. Whether you're an old hand at slinging JavaScript or a newcomer to the frontend world, this book has something for you.

The Goal of This Book

The list of requirements for frontend work keeps increasing. You now need to build websites that load quickly on shaky connections, render perfectly on mobile devices, and respond with lightning speed to user input. All of these tasks require dealing with a high number of events from disparate sources, be it your CRM, late-breaking news, or just a chat room. The topic of this book, observables, is a new way of thinking about managing these events, even when they may occur sometime in the future. Observables are a neat concept, but what's important is that you can keep things straight in your head, allowing you to build bigger, faster, and less-buggy applications for your users.

It's important to ask, with such a big claim as "simplifying frontend development," what exactly is simplified? While RxJS (short for "Reactive eXtensions to JavaScript") brings simplicity to many areas, this book focuses on two areas that can have you reaching for the aspirin time and time again:

Asynchronous Calls and Control Flow

JavaScript's async-first design has been both a blessing and a curse. While the event loop allows us to fire off AJAX calls with ease, keeping track of them all can be quite the chore. A single AJAX request can be modeled as a promise, but more than one suddenly means there's a cacophony of items to manually track (and even cancel) as the user progresses through our app. One of the most notorious examples, the typeahead, will be covered in *Advanced Async*. You'll learn how to delegate both the calls and control flow to RxJS, allowing you to focus on the rest of your application.

State Management

On the other hand, managing an application's state has been the bane of programmers since RAM was invented, leading to the oft-quoted advice to "turn it off and on again," resetting the computer's state. JavaScript makes this worse by defaulting to a global, mutable state. In recent years, the JavaScript community has started to build some impressive solutions to this problem.

RxJS compartmentalizes your eventing flows, encapsulating each action in a single function. Building on top of this, RxJS also provides many helper operators that keep an internal state, allowing you to outsource your state worries to the library. In addition to these operators, you'll learn about ngrx, a state management library built on top of RxJS in *Advanced Angular*. In *Reactive Game Development*, you'll build out your own state system that's specific to the HTML5 Canvas API.

 Joe asks:
Why RxJS over Other Observable Libraries?

RxJS is just one of many different JavaScript libraries that implement the observable pattern. RxJS is one of the oldest, and as of this writing, has had six major releases. It's also one of the most popular observable tools, which means that there will be plenty of StackOverflow questions, blog posts, and yes, books about it, if you run into trouble. RxJS goes for the "batteries included" philosophy, so any conceivable method or pattern you need, RxJS will have it. It also includes tooling for you to create your own observables as needed. RxJS is built on TypeScript, allowing editors like Visual Studio Code to take advantage of type hinting to point out bugs as soon as possible. Finally, it's the backbone for the popular Angular framework, a topic we'll cover later on (though RxJS is by no means exclusive to Angular).

Other JavaScript libraries that implement the observable pattern include mobx, BaconJS, and Kefir. These either focus on a specific use case for observables (like mobx and state management) or prefer a limited feature set to focus on performance (though RxJS is very fast, especially the latest version).

But I Already Use (Insert Framework Here)!

Don't worry! RxJS is not intended to replace your entire frontend toolset. Rather, it's been designed to integrate with whatever JavaScript framework you use, be it a tangled mess of jQuery and twine, or the latest framework that was just released this week. The Angular framework in particular has decided to integrate with RxJS out-of-the-box, and this book covers some of those scenarios, but the knowledge contained in this book is by no means specific to Angular.

How to Read This Book

This book intends to default to the practical. Everyone learns best by doing, and so each chapter is a series of projects for you to build, each one illustrating a new concept for you to learn. The projects start out small (the first one's just a stopwatch) but grow in complexity. Before you know it, you'll be building entire websites backed by the impressive power of RxJS. This is not a book to be read from cover to cover in one sitting; rather it's a companion, meant to be cracked open on a second monitor as you type away, building out one of the many examples.

If you're a complete newcomer to the world of observables, I'd recommend starting at the beginning of this book and working your way through. If you've subscribed to an observable or two, you may want to skip ahead to *Managing Asynchronous Events*, though the interim chapters might be a good refresher.

This book is split into three sections, each building on concepts introduced in the previous sections.

Section 1: Vanilla RxJS

This section starts off with an introduction to observables and how to create them in RxJS. It focuses on teaching the concepts behind RxJS, so that you're more familiar with what's going on. You'll learn the concepts and best practices behind observables while tackling ever-harder examples. This section is framework-agnostic, so it will be equally useful to you regardless of your preferred toolset.

Section 2: RxJS in Angular

As incredible as RxJS is, it works best as a glue that holds the rest of the application together. An application built entirely of glue is not a good application. In this section, you'll dive into RxJS' use in Angular, building entire websites. You'll see how RxJS integrates into Angular to simplify tasks both complicated and repetitive. You'll also move beyond pure coding to see how RxJS use can enable us to build much more effective user experience. This section ends with a performance profiling task, where you'll use RxJS to update a page only when it's absolutely needed.

Section 3: Reactive Game Development

In this final section, you'll construct your own game based on the Canvas API. Games have an incredible amount of things going on at any given moment, so RxJS is a perfect fit for organizing all of the hectic events that might be triggering. This is also the most advanced section, where you'll build your own reusable observable operator alongside a from-scratch state management tool.

Setting Up the Environment

To use this book, you'll need the following (older versions of node/npm may work, but they haven't been tested):

- NodeJS version 10.1.0 or greater
- npm version 6.1.0 or greater
- The code found on the page for this book at The Pragmatic Bookshelf site[1]

Download the zipped code from this book's page and unzip it. You'll find four folders—three corresponding to one of the three sections in this book and an asset server.

- The vanilla folder contains the relevant code and scaffolding for the first five chapters that cover the RxJS library in depth.

- ng2 covers the next three chapters, which are an overview for using RxJS within the Angular framework.

- canvas contains the code and other related files to build your first RxJS-based game.

The asset-server folder contains a local server you'll use to serve assets throughout the book. Once you've unzipped the code, run npm install in the asset-server folder to ensure all dependencies are installed. When everything is installed, run npm start to start the server, which will be listening at http://localhost:3000. You'll use this server throughout the book.

Section-specific instructions for using the code provided is at the beginning of each section.

Typescript

The code in this book, as well as all the examples, use TypeScript, a language that is a superset of JavaScript that adds optional types. No TypeScript

---

1. https://pragprog.com/titles/rkrxjs/source_code

knowledge is needed to start this book. Everything you need to know will be explained along the way.

TypeScript can't be run directly, so a compile step is needed. The code in this book is configured to use SystemJS to compile your code behind the scenes, so you don't need to worry about it. You may want to install language support into your editor of choice, though this is not required.

Why TypeScript?

In vanilla JavaScript, the following is perfectly valid syntax:

```
function canRegister(age) {
  return age > 13;
}

let user = {
  name: 'Jose',
  age: 23
};

canRegister(user);
```

This code prevents poor Jose from using our site, despite the fact that he's well over the minimum required age. The bug here is a *type mismatch*. The function canRegister was expecting a number, but was passed an object. Java-Script helpfully tries to make up for our crass mistake, sees an object used against >—an operator that expects a number, and converts that object to a number: NaN. What if we could discover innocuous bugs like this without even leaving our editor (and more importantly, before our users do)?

A superset of JavaScript, TypeScript adds optional types into JavaScript. We can add an optional type notation to canRegister that explicitly notes that can-Register is looking for a numerical type.

```
function canRegister(age: number) {
  return age > 13;
}

let user = {
  name: 'Jose',
  age: 23
};

canRegister(user);
```

In any editor with a TypeScript plugin, this will immediately reveal the bug. TypeScript knows the type of user is "an object with a name property set to a string, and an age property set to a number." If we try to pass that through to a function that just wants a number, the type mismatch is revealed. While it's possible to write Angular code in regular JavaScript, TypeScript is strongly recommended, and what we'll use here.

```
  3  ⊟ function canRegister(age: number) {
  4        return age > 13;
  5    }
  6
  7  ⊟ let user = {
  8        name: 'Jose',
  9        age: 23
 10    };
 11
 12    canRegister(user);
```
(1/1) [ts] Argument of type '{ name: string; age: number; }' is not assignable to parameter of type 'number'.

You don't need to know anything about TypeScript to read this book. All of the compilation will be handled for you as part of the code included in this book.

Experimenting in the Sandbox

You may wish to travel off the beaten path and experiment with RxJS as you learn about various aspects of RxJS. The sandbox.ts file has been set up for this purpose (with a link to the corresponding HTML file from the project homepage). All of RxJS is available, so feel free to play around with whatever you like. To view the sandbox in your browser, start the server as mentioned above and browse to http://localhost:8081/sandbox/sandbox.html.

Online Resources

Visit this book's online home,[2] where you'll find errata and any source code you need.

Acknowledgments

Thanks to Kevin W. Beam, Alex Bezek, Nathan Brenner, Nick Capito, Chad Dumler-Montplaisir, Kevin Gisi, Steve Hill, Daivid Morgan, Peter Perlepes, and Stephen Wolff for reviewing early copies of this book. Thanks to Pascal Precht and Jurgen Van de Moere for all their writing and blogging about Angular and observables that taught me so much. Special thanks also goes to Rob Wormald for selflessly helping me when I was struggling to first learn RxJS. I'd also like to thank my editor, Brian MacDonald, for putting up with the many beginner mistakes I made during the development of this book.

2.	https://pragprog.com/book/rkrxjs/build-reactive-websites-with-rxjs

CHAPTER 1

Creating Observables

If you're brand new to the concepts in observables or just need a refresher, this is the chapter for you. This chapter starts with a sense of where observables conceptually fit in the greater world of JavaScript tools. You'll build your first project of the book: a stopwatch. A stopwatch may seem simple, but you'll need to learn several key observable concepts to get it working. Once the stopwatch is up and running, you will prove the reusability of Rx by building a drag-and-drop example from the stopwatch code using the exact same pattern and operators. First things first, though, it's time for Rx basics.

Using the Code Provided for This Section

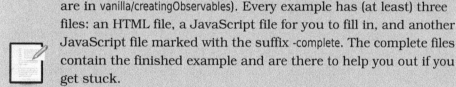 The files you'll edit in this section's examples are located in the vanilla directory, organized by chapter (so this chapter's examples are in vanilla/creatingObservables). Every example has (at least) three files: an HTML file, a JavaScript file for you to fill in, and another JavaScript file marked with the suffix -complete. The complete files contain the finished example and are there to help you out if you get stuck.

To set up the server for this chapter's code, make sure you're in the vanilla directory and run npm install. When that's complete, run npm start to get the Webpack dev server going. To get started, open your browser to http://localhost:8081.

Introducing Rx Concepts

First, we need to figure out where observables stand in the greater context of JavaScript land. This is a variable:

```
let myVar = 42;
```

As you probably know, a variable contains a single value and that value can be used immediately after declaration. Variables are pretty simple. On the other hand, we have arrays:

```
let myArr = [42, 'hello world', NaN];
```

This array represents a *collection* of values. Like the humble variable, an array also contains its data at the moment of creation. If all of programming just used these two concepts, life would be pretty easy. Everything needed to run a program would be immediately available when the program started. Unfortunately, there are times when the data the program needs isn't immediately available. For instance, a web page might need to make an AJAX request to get information about the current user:

```
let user = getUserFromAPI();
doSomething(user);
```

Running this code results in a fireball of cataclysmic proportions or a stack trace. Either is likely (though it's probably the stack trace). In any case, what it doesn't get is our data, since the request has been made to the backend but hasn't finished yet. One possible solution to this problem is to stop the entire process and do *nothing* until the AJAX request returns. This is silly. If my wife asks me to unload the groceries when she returns from the store, the proper answer is not to sit absolutely still on the couch until she arrives. Instead, I make a mental note that I have a task to do some time in the future. The JavaScript version of this mental note is called a promise:

```
let userRequest = getUserFromAPI();
```

Like a variable, userRequest contains a single value, but it doesn't immediately have that value. A promise *represents* data that has been requested but isn't there yet. To do anything with that data, we need to *unwrap* the promise using the .then method:

```
let userRequest = getUserFromAPI();
userRequest.then(userData => {
  // Called when the request returns
  processUser(userData);
});
```

Acting as a "mental note," a promise allows the core process to go on doing things elsewhere, while the backend rustles through various database indexes looking for our user. Once the request returns, our process peeks inside the .then to see what to do, executing whatever function we passed in.

So far we've covered:

	Sync	Async
Single	Variable	Promise
Collection	Array	???

The remaining piece in the puzzle is the topic of this book: The observable. Observables are like arrays in that they represent a *collection* of events, but are also like promises in that they're asynchronous: each event in the collection arrives at some indeterminate point in the future. This is distinct from a collection of promises (like Promise.all) in that an observable can handle an arbitrary number of events, and a promise can only track one thing. An observable can be used to model clicks of a button. It represents all the clicks that will happen over the lifetime of the application, but the clicks will happen at some point in the future that we can't predict.

```
let myObs$ = clicksOnButton(myButton);
```

Joe asks:
Why Is There a Dollar Sign?

You'll notice that there's an odd dollar sign hanging onto the end of the variable name. This is a convention in the Rx world that indicates that the variable in question is an observable. This convention is used throughout the book, and you're encouraged to use it in your own work (though it's by no means mandatory).

These clicks will happen over the lifetime of the application (imagine designing a web app that expects every click to happen at once!). Much like a promise, we need to unwrap our observable to access the values it contains. The observable unwrapping method is called subscribe. The function passed into subscribe is called every time the observable emits a value. (In this case, a message is logged to the console anytime the button is clicked.)

```
let myObs$ = clicksOnButton(myButton);
myObs$
.subscribe(clickEvent => console.log('The button was clicked!'));
```

One thing to note here is that observables under RxJS are *lazy*. This means that if there's no subscribe call on myObs$, no click event handler is created. Observables only run when they know someone's listening in to the data they're emitting.

Building a Stopwatch

Enough theory—you're probably itching to start building something. The first project you'll take on in this book is a stopwatch that contains three observables. The stopwatch will have two buttons, one for starting and one for stopping, with an observable monitoring each. Behind the scenes will be a third observable, ticking away the seconds since the start button was pressed in increments of 1/10th of a second. This observable will be hooked up to a counter on the page. You'll learn how to create observables that take input from the user, as well as observables that interact with the DOM to display the latest state of your app.

Before we get to the code, take a second to think about how you'd implement this without Rx. There'd be a couple of click handlers for the start and stop buttons. At some point, the program would create an interval to count the seconds. Sketch out the program structure—what order do these events happen in? Did you remember to clear the interval after the stop button was pressed? Is business logic clearly separated from the view? Typically, these aren't concerns for an app of this size; I'm specifically calling them out now, so you can see how Rx handles them in a simple stopwatch. Later on, you'll use the same techniques on much larger projects, without losing clarity.

This project has two different categories of observables. The interval timer has its own internal state and outputs to the document object model (DOM). The two-click streams will be attached to the buttons and won't have any kind of internal state. Let's tackle the hardest part first—the interval timer behind the scenes that needs to maintain state.

Running a Timer

This timer will need to track the total number of seconds elapsed and emit the latest value every 1/10th of a second. When the stop button is pressed, the interval should be cancelled. We'll need an observable for this, leading to the question: "How on earth do I build an observable?"

Good question—read through this example (don't worry about knowing everything that's going on, but take a few guesses as you go through it).

```
import { Observable } from 'rxjs';

let tenthSecond$ = new Observable(observer => {
  let counter = 0;
  observer.next(counter);
  let interv = setInterval(() => {
    counter++;
    observer.next(counter);
  }, 100);

  return function unsubscribe() { clearInterval(interv); };
});
```

Let's walk through that line-by-line. As you read through each snippet of code, add it to the stopwatch.ts file in vanilla/creatingObservables.

```
import { Observable } from 'rxjs';
```

The first thing is to use import to bring in Observable from the RxJS library. All of the projects in this book start off by bringing in the components needed to run the project. If your editor is TypeScript-aware (I recommend Visual Studio Code[1]), you probably have the option to automatically import things as you type. Most examples in this book skip the import statement for brevity's sake.

```
let tenthSecond$ = new Observable(observer => {
```

There's that dollar sign again, indicating the variable contains an observable. On the other side of the equals sign is the standard Rx constructor for observables, which takes a single argument: a function with a single parameter, an observer. Technically, an *observer* is any object that has the following methods: next(someItem) (called to pass the latest value to the observable stream), error(someError) (called when something goes wrong), and complete() (called once the data source has no more information to pass on). In the case of the observable constructor function, Rx creates the observer for you and passes it to the inner function. Later on, we'll see some other places you can use observers and even create new ones.

```
let counter = 0;
observer.next(counter);
let interv = setInterval(() => {
  counter++;
  observer.next(counter);
}, 100);
```

---

1. https://code.visualstudio.com/

While setInterval isn't perfect at keeping exact time, it suffices for this example. You'll learn about more detailed methods of tracking time in *Advanced Angular*.

Inside the constructor function, things get interesting. There's an internal state in the counter variable that tracks the number of tenths-of-a-second since the start. Immediately, observer.next is called with the initial value of 0. Then there's an interval that fires every 100 ms, incrementing the counter and calling observer.next(counter). This .next method on the observer is how an observable announces to the subscriber that it has a new value available for consumption. The practical upshot is that this observable emits an integer every 100 ms representing how many deciseconds have elapsed since…

…well, when exactly does this function *run*? Throw some console.log statements in and run the above snippet. What happens?

Nothing appears in the console—the constructor appears to never actually run. This is the lazy observable at work. In Rx land, this constructor function will only run when someone subscribes to it. Not only that, but if there's a *second* subscriber, all of this will run a second time, creating an entirely separate stream (this means that each subscriber gets its own timer)! You can learn more about how all of this works in *Multiplexing Observables*, but for now, just remember that each subscription creates a new stream.

Finally, the inner function returns yet another function (called an *unsubscribe* function):

```
return function unsubscribe() { clearInterval(interv); };
```

If the constructor function returns another function, this inner function runs whenever a listener unsubscribes from the source observable. In this case, the interval is no longer needed, so we clear it. This saves CPU cycles, which keeps fans from spinning up on the desktop, and mobile users will thank us for sparing their batteries. Remember, each subscriber gets their own instance of the constructor, and so, has their own cleanup function. All of the setup and teardown logic is located in the same place, so it requires less mental overhead to remember to clean up all the objects that get created.

Speaking of mental overhead, that was a lot of information in just a few lines of code. There are a lot of new concepts here, and it might get tedious writing this every time we want an interval. Fortunately, all of this work has already been implemented in the Rx library in the form of a *creation operator*:

```
import { interval } from 'rxjs';

let tenthSecond$ = interval(100);
```

Rx ships with a whole bunch of these creation operators for common tasks. You can find the complete list under the "Static Method Summary" heading at the official RxJS site.[2] interval(100) is similar to the big constructor function we had above. Now, to actually run this code, subscribe:

```
import { interval } from 'rxjs';

let tenthSecond$ = interval(100);
tenthSecond$.subscribe(console.log);
```

When there's a subscribe call, numbers start being logged to the console. The numbers that are logged are *slightly* off from what we want. The current implementation counts the number of tenths-of-a-second since the subscription, not the number of seconds. One way to fix that is to modify the constructor function, but stuffing all the logic into the constructor function gets unwieldy. Instead, an observable stream modifies data after a root observable emits it using a tool called an *operator*.

Piping Data Through Operators

An operator is a tool provided by RxJS that allows you to manipulate the data in the observable as it streams through. You can import operators from 'rxjs/operators'. To use an operator, pass it into the .pipe method of an observable. Here, the fictional exampleOperator is used for illustration:

```
import { interval } from 'rxjs';
import { exampleOperator } from 'rxjs/operators';

interval(100)
.pipe(
  exampleOperator()
);
```

 In previous versions of RxJS, the operators were methods attached directly to the observable. This made it difficult for bundling tools like Webpack to determine which operators weren't needed in the production bundle. With RxJS v6, only operators that are needed are imported, allowing a bundler to ignore the rest, resulting in a smaller bundle.

Next, you'll learn how to use the most popular operator: map.

---

2.   http://reactivex.io/rxjs/class/es6/Observable.js~Observable.html

Manipulating Data in Flight with map

Right now, you have a collection of almost-right data that needs just one little tweak for it to be correct. Enter the map operator.

Generally speaking, a *map* function takes two parameters (a collection and another function), applies the function to each item, and returns a *new* collection containing the results. A simple implementation looks something like this:

```
function map(oldArr, someFunc) {
  let newArr = [];
  for (let i = 0; i < oldArr.length; i++) {
    newArr.push(someFunc(oldArr[i]));
  }
  return newArr;
}
```

JavaScript provides a built-in map for arrays that only takes a single parameter (the function). The array in question is the one the map method is called on:

```
let newArr = oldArr.map(someFunc);
```

This example only works with synchronous arrays—conceptually, map works on any type of collection. Observables are just such a collection and Rx provides a map operator of its own. It's piped through a source observable, takes a function, and returns a new observable that emits the result of the passed-in function. Importantly, the modification in map is *synchronous*. Even though new data arrives over time, this map immediately modifies the data and passes it on. Syntax-wise, the only major difference is that the RxJS example uses pipe to pass in map:

```
let newObservable$ = oldObservable$.pipe(
  map(someFunc)
);
```

We can apply this mapping concept to tenthSecond$. The source observable will be the interval created earlier. The modification is to divide the incoming number by 10. The result looks something like:

```
import { map } from 'rxjs/operators';

tenthSecond$
.pipe(
  map(num => num / 10)
)
.subscribe(console.log);
```

With these few lines, the first observable is ready. Two more to go.

Wait, What's That with the Log?

You might be thrown by the idea of passing console.log directly into the subscribe function like that. subscribe expects a function, which it calls every time with whatever value comes next in the observable. console.log is just such a function. This setup is the equivalent of value => console.log(value), but it saves us some typing. If you're on an older browser, this might cause errors. In that case, use the full function value => console.log(value) and make a note to upgrade to a modern browser as soon as you can.

Handling User Input

The next step is to manage clicks on the start and stop buttons. First, grab the elements off the page with querySelector:

```
let startButton = document.querySelector('#start-button');
let stopButton = document.querySelector('#stop-button');
```

Now that we have buttons, we need to figure out when the user clicks them. You could use the constructor covered in the last section to build an observable that streams click events from an arbitrary element:

```
function trackClickEvents(element) {
  return new Observable(observer => {
    let emitClickEvent = event => observer.next(event);

    element.addEventListener('click', emitClickEvent);
    return () => element.removeEventListener(emitClickEvent);
  });
}
```

Much like interval, we can let the library do all the work for us. Rx provides a fromEvent creation operator for exactly this case. It takes a DOM element (or other event-emitting object) and an event name as parameters and returns a stream that fires whenever the event fires on the element. Using the buttons from above:

```
import { fromEvent } from 'rxjs';

let startButton = document.querySelector('#start-button');
let stopButton = document.querySelector('#stop-button')

let startClick$ = fromEvent(startButton, 'click');
let stopClick$ = fromEvent(stopButton, 'click');
```

Add a pair of subscribes to the above example to make sure everything's working. Every time you click, you should see a click event object logged to the console. If you don't, make sure the code subscribes to the correct observable and that you're clicking on the correct button.

Assembling the Stopwatch

All three observables have been created. Now it's time to assemble everything into an actual program.

vanilla/creatingObservables/stopwatch-complete.ts

```
// Imports
import { interval, fromEvent } from 'rxjs';
import { map, takeUntil } from 'rxjs/operators';

// Elements
let startButton = document.querySelector('#start-button');
let stopButton = document.querySelector('#stop-button');
let resultsArea = document.querySelector<HTMLElement>('.output');
// Observables
let tenthSecond$ = interval(100);
let startClick$ = fromEvent(startButton, 'click');
let stopClick$ = fromEvent(stopButton, 'click');

startClick$.subscribe(() => {
  tenthSecond$
    .pipe(
      map(item => (item / 10)),
      takeUntil(stopClick$)
    )
    .subscribe(num => resultsArea.innerText = num + 's');
});
```

> \|/   **Joe asks:**
> ʔϛ   **What's that <HTMLElement> mean?**
>
> This book uses TypeScript for all the examples. The <angle bracket notation> denotes the specific return type for querySelector. TypeScript knows that querySelector will return some kind of Element. In this case, we know specifically that we're querying for an element of the HTML variety, so we use this syntax to override the generic element. With that override, TypeScript now knows that resultsArea has properties specific to an HTMLElement, such as .innerText. We don't need to use the angle brackets when we query for button elements, because we're not doing anything button specific with those variables, so the generic Element type suffices.

There's a few new concepts in the stopwatch example, so let's take it blow-by-blow. To start, there are six variables, three elements from the page and three observables (you can tell which ones are observables, because we annotated the variable name with a dollar sign). The first line of business logic is a subscription to startClick$, which creates a click event handler on that element. At this point, no one's clicked the Start button, so Rx hasn't created the interval or an event listener for the stop button (saving CPU cycles without extra work on your part).

When the Start button is clicked, the subscribe function is triggered (there's a new event). The actual click event is ignored, as this implementation doesn't care about the specifics of the click, just that it happened. Immediately, tenthSecond$ runs its constructor (creating an interval behind the scenes), because there's a subscribe call at the end of the inner chain. Every event fired by $tenthSecond runs through the map function, dividing each number by 10. Suddenly, an unexpected operator appears in the form of takeUntil.

takeUntil is an operator that attaches itself to an observable stream and *takes* values from that stream *until* the observable that's passed in as an argument emits a value. At that point, takeUntil unsubscribes from both. In this case, we want to continue listening to new events from the timer observable until the user clicks the Stop button. When the Stop button is pressed, Rx cleans up both the interval *and* the Stop button click handler. This means that both the subscribe and unsubscribe calls for stopClick$ happen at the library level. This helps keep the implementation simple, but it's important to remember that the (un)subscribing is still happening.

Finally, we put the latest value from tenthSecond$ on the page in the subscribe call. Putting the business logic in Rx and updating the view in the subscribe call is a common pattern you'll see in both this book and in any observable-heavy frontend application.

You'll notice that repeated clicks on the Start button cause multiple streams to start. The inner stream should listen for clicks on either button and pass that to takeUntil. This involves combining two streams into one, a technique you'll learn in *Manipulating Streams*.

How Does This Apply Externally?

I'm sure you're just *jaw-droppingly stunned* at the amazing wonder of a stopwatch. Even in this basic example, you should start to see how Rx can simplify our complicated frontend codebases. Each call is cleanly separated, and the view update has a single location. While it provides a neat demo, modern websites aren't made entirely of stopwatches, so why build one at all?

The patterns in this example didn't just solve the mystery of the stopwatch. Everything you've built so far in this chapter sums into a pattern that solves any problem of the shape, "Upon an initiating event, watch a stream of data until a concluding event occurs." This means that this code also solves one of the biggest frontend frustrations:

Drag and Drop

Another example of RxJS's power is drag-and-drop. Anyone who's tried to implement drag-and-drop without a library understands just how hair-pullingly frustrating it is. The concept is simple: On a mousedown event, track movement and update the page with the new position of the dragged item until the user lets go of the mouse button. The difficult part of dealing with a dragged element comes in tracking all of the events that fire, maintaining state and order without devolving into a horrible garbled mess of code.

Adding to the confusion, a flick of the user's wrist can generate thousands of mousemove events—so the code *must* be performant. Rx's lazy subscription model means that we aren't tracking any mousemove events until the user actually drags the element. Additionally, mousemove events are fired synchronously, so Rx will guarantee that they arrive in order to the next step in the stream.

Write out the following snippet in dragdrop.ts, in the same directory as the previous stopwatch example. The following example reuses the stopwatch patterns to create a draggable tool:

vanilla/creatingObservables/dragdrop-complete.ts

```
import { fromEvent } from 'rxjs';
import { map, takeUntil } from 'rxjs/operators';

let draggable = <HTMLElement>document.querySelector('#draggable');

let mouseDown$ = fromEvent<MouseEvent>(draggable, 'mousedown');
let mouseMove$ = fromEvent<MouseEvent>(document, 'mousemove');
let mouseUp$ = fromEvent<MouseEvent>(document, 'mouseup');

mouseDown$.subscribe(() => {
  mouseMove$
  .pipe(
    map(event => {
      event.preventDefault();
      return {
        x: event.clientX,
        y: event.clientY
      };
    }),
    takeUntil(mouseUp$)
  )
  .subscribe(pos => {
    // Draggable is absolutely positioned
    draggable.style.left = pos.x + 'px';
    draggable.style.top = pos.y + 'px';
  });
});
```

At the start are the same bunch of variable declarations that you saw in the stopwatch example. In this case, the code tracks a few events on the entire HTML document, though if only one element is a valid area for dragging, that could be passed in. The initiating observable, mouseDown$ is subscribed. In the subscription, each mouseMove$ event is mapped, so that the only data passed on are the current coordinates of the mouse. takeUntil is used so that once the mouse button is released, everything's cleaned up. Finally, the inner subscribe updates the position of the dragged element across the page.

Plenty of other conceptual models lend themselves to this pattern.

Loading Bars

Instead of trying to track lots of global state, let Rx do the heavy lifting. You'll find out in *Managing Asynchronous Events* how to add a single function here to handle cases when a bit of your app didn't load.

```
startLoad$.subscribe(() => {
  assetPipeline$
  .pipe(
    takeUntil(stopLoad$)
  )
  .subscribe(item => updateLoader(item));
});
```

Chat Rooms

We both know just how much programmers love chat rooms. Here, we use the power of Rx to track only the rooms the user has joined. You'll use some of these techniques to build an entire chat application in *Multiplexing Observables*.

```
loadRoom$.subscribe(() => {
  chatStream$
  .pipe(
    takeUntil(roomLeave$)
  )
  .subscribe(msg => addMsgToRoom(msg));
});
```

Using a Subscription

There's one more vocabulary word before this chapter is over: *subscription*. While piping through an *operator* returns an observable:

```
let someNewObservable$ = anObservable$.pipe(
  map(x => x * 2)
);
```

a call to .subscribe returns a Subscription:

```
let aSubscription = someNewObservable$.subscribe(console.log);
```

Subscriptions are not a subclass of observables, so there's no dollar sign at the end of the variable name. Rather, a subscription is used to keep track of a specific subscription to that observable. This means whenever the program no longer needs the values from that particular observable stream, it can use the subscription to unsubscribe from all future events:

```
aSubscription.unsubscribe();
```

Some operators, like takeUntil above, handle subscriptions internally. Most of the time, your code manages subscriptions manually. We cover this in detail in *Managing Asynchronous Events*. You can also "merge" subscriptions together or even add custom unsubscription logic. I recommend that you keep all logic related to subscribing and unsubscribing in the constructor function if possible, so that consumers of your observable don't need to worry about cleanup.

```
// Combine multiple subscriptions
aSubscription.add(bSubscription);
aSubscription.add(cSubscription);

// Add a custom function that's called on unsubscribe
aSubscription.add(() => {
  console.log('Custom unsubscribe function');
});

// Calls all three unsubscribes and the custom function
aSubscription.unsubscribe();
```

Experimenting with Observables

You've only dipped your toes into the massive toolbox Rx provides. Read on to learn about operators beyond map and takeUntil. map has worked for everything so far, but what happens when we throw an asynchronous wrench in the works or tackle multiple operations inside?

This section covers the of constructor and the take and delay operators. They're included in the first chapter, because all three are useful for hands-on experimentation with observables. If you're not quite sure how an operator works, these tools let you get an easily-understood observable stream up and running to test the confusing operator.

of

The of constructor allows for easy creation of an observable out of a known data source. It takes any number of arguments and returns an observable containing each argument as a separate event. The following example logs the three strings passed in as separate events.

```
import { of } from 'rxjs';

of('hello', 'world', '!')
.subscribe(console.log);
```

The of constructor can be handy when you try to learn a new operator; it's the simplest way to create an observable of arbitrary data. For instance, if you're struggling with the map operator, it may be elucidating to pass a few strings through to see what gets logged.

```
import { of } from 'rxjs';

of('foo', 'bar', 'baz')
.pipe(
  map(word => word.split(''))
)
.subscribe(console.log);
```

Beyond learning RxJS, the of constructor is used when testing observables, as it allows you to pass in precise data during unit testing.

The take Operator

Earlier in this chapter, you took a look at takeUntil, which continued taking events until the passed-in observable emitted a value. The take operator is related to that, but it simplifies things. It's passed a single integer argument, and takes that many events from the observable before it unsubscribes.

```
import { interval } from 'rxjs';
import { take } from 'rxjs/operators';

// interval is an infinite observable
interval(1000)
.pipe(
  // take transforms that into an observable of only three items
  take(3)
)
// Logs 0, 1, 2 as separate events and then completes
.subscribe(console.log);
```

take is useful when you only want the first slice of an observable's data. In practical terms, this helps in situations where you only want to be notified on the first click on a button, but don't care about subsequent clicks. Another example is a trivia game where only the first three players to submit an answer get the points.

```
answer$
.pipe(
  filter(isAnswerCorrect),
  take(3)
)
.subscribe(updateScore);
```

It's also helpful to use the take operator in combination with interval when debugging as an easy way to create a finite, asynchronous stream.

The delay Operator

The delay operator is passed an integer argument and delays all events coming through the observable chain by that many milliseconds. This example logs 1, 2, and 3 one second after the code is executed.

```
of(1,2,3)
.pipe(
  delay(1000)
)
.subscribe(console.log);
```

Like the other two tools here, delay helps you manipulate your experimental streams to play with observables and their operators. The delay operator is also helpful when connecting multiple streams together (this example uses merge, an operator/constructor combo you'll learn about in *Manipulating Streams*).

```
import { of, merge } from 'rxjs';
import { delay } from 'rxjs/operators';

let oneSecond$ = of('one').pipe(delay(1000));
let twoSecond$ = of('two').pipe(delay(2000));
let threeSecond$ = of('three').pipe(delay(3000));
let fourSecond$ = of('four').pipe(delay(4000));

merge(
  oneSecond$,
  twoSecond$,
  threeSecond$,
  fourSecond$
)
.subscribe(console.log);
```

Connecting the Dots

What does this example log, and when?

vanilla/creatingObservables/connectingDots-complete.ts

```
import { interval } from 'rxjs';
import { take, map, delay} from 'rxjs/operators';

interval(1000)
  .pipe(
    take(5),
    map(val => val * 5),
    delay(500)
  )
  .subscribe(console.log);

Answer:
1500ms: logs 0
2500ms: logs 5
3500ms: logs 10
4500ms: logs 15
5500ms: logs 20 (and finishes)
```

What We Learned

You've now seen how observables work at the basic level, and you've grasped the vocabulary surrounding them. Don't worry if you're still unclear about the specifics. The principles introduced here will come up again and again, so there will be plenty of opportunities to practice. On the other hand, if you're looking for a challenge, implement a lap button on the stopwatch. Clicking a lap button pauses the rendering of the view but doesn't pause the internal counter. Clicking the lap button again shows the current counter state.

Now that you know how to create streams of data with observables, it's time to learn more about how to modify the data within a stream. In the next chapter, you go on beyond map to learn about many more operators that will be foundational to your RxJS knowledge.

CHAPTER 2

Manipulating Streams

In the last chapter, you learned how to create observables with new Observable, along with a few of the helper operators Rx provides. You also peeked into the world of manipulating values in an observable stream with the magic of map. While mapping is a common pattern, the Rx library has many other operators for working with in-stream data. In fact, most Rx work is about manipulating the data as it comes down the stream. This change can be in the form of manipulating the data directly (map), changing the timing of the data (delay), or operating on the observables themselves (takeUntil).

This chapter expands your knowledge of the types of map functions available and adds several new types of operators to your tool belt:

- mergeMap combines flattening and mapping into a single operation.
- filter allows a stream to be picky about what values are allowed.
- The tap operator is a unique case that doesn't manipulate the stream's values directly, but allows a developer to tap into the stream and debug it.

The first of two projects in this chapter is a Pig Latin translator. Through this translator, you'll learn how to manipulate values as they pass through an observable stream. The second project, a typeahead tool, takes the concepts from the Pig Latin translator and builds a more complicated tool out of them, teaching you how to debug in-flight data.

Translating Pig Latin with Flatten and Reduce

Pig Latin[1] is a silly pseudolanguage based on English. Translating an English sentence into Pig Latin is simple. Split each sentence into words and put each word through the following modifications:

---

1. https://en.wikipedia.org/wiki/Pig_Latin

- Remove the first letter of each word: "Pig Latin" becomes "ig atin" (exception: ignore single-letter words)

- Add the first letter removed in the previous step plus 'ay' to the end of the word: "ig-pay atin-lay"

Alas, nothing is ever that simple, and there's an edge case we need to worry about: single-letter words (specifically, a and I). To keep it simple, in the event of a single-letter word, our code will let it be and return the word unchanged.

Advanced Pig Latin

 Like any natural language, there are many dialects of Pig Latin. Some break things down further, checking whether the word starts with a consonant or a vowel. We're just using a simplified Pig Latin as an example here. If you want to add more rules after you finish this section, go for it!

Pig Latin is enormous fun to say aloud. Some folks are even able to have full conversations in it without missing a beat. On the other hand, we want to write a program to do all that work for us. Translating the single-word rules to JavaScript results in this function:

```
// Converts a word in English to one in Pig Latin
function pigLatinify(word) {
  // Handle single-letter case and empty strings
  if (word.length < 2) {
    return word;
  }
  return word.slice(1) + '-' + word[0].toLowerCase() + 'ay';
}
```

You can use the techniques from the last chapter (fromEvent and map) to connect this function to a textbox that prints out a Pig Latin translation on every keystroke:

```
let keyUp$ = fromEvent(textbox, 'keyup')
.pipe(
  map(event => event.target.value),
  map(wordString => wordString.split(/\s+/)),
  map(wordArray => wordArray.map(pigLatinify))
)
.subscribe(translated => console.log(translated));
```

A quick review: Every keyup event is sent down the stream by the fromEvent constructor. The first map extracts the value of the textbox. The second splits the string using a regex that matches one or more instances of whitespace (\s: match whitespace, +: one or more instances). The final map takes the array of words and passes each word through the translation function (using Array.prototype.map).

> ## Chaining Operators
>
> In the previous example, technically, three map operators could be combined into a single (if somewhat complex) operator:
>
> ```
> map(event => event.target.value.split(/\s+/).map(pigLatinify))
> ```
>
> In fact, in older versions of Rx, munging everything together into a single operator would increase performance at the cost of readability, because every operator technically created a new observable at the library layer. Version 5 (and beyond) of RxJS solved that problem—in the case of combinable operators, RxJS merges the functions at the library level, improving performance without sacrificing simplicity. A win all around.

The three-map snippet works just fine, but it's only one of many possible ways to implement a real-time translator. In the next section, you'll see some new techniques used to the same effect, but they provide building blocks that the rest of the book will expand on. The first of these is the idea of function that flattens multidimensional collections so we can better handle that array of words.

Flattening

You may have heard of a "flatten" function. Flatten functions take an input of some sort and "unwrap" it. (In this case, *unwrapping* an array is to pull out the elements in the array and use those.) This hypothetical code snippet returns [2, 4, 7, 12]:

```
flatten([[2], [4, 7], 12])
```

Usually, a single call to flatten only unwraps by one layer. Flatten iterates through the array, unwrapping each item if possible. The element 12 cannot be unwrapped, so flatten uses the raw value in the resulting collection. Flatten can be used with more than arrays—promises and observables also can be unwrapped by passing along the data within rather than the abstraction. Promise.all is a type of flatten, taking an array of promises and returning a single promise that contains an array of all of the resulting data:

```
Promise.all([
  fetch('/endpoint/productA'),
  fetch('/endpoint/productB'),
  fetch('/endpoint/productC')
])
.then(arrayOfProducts => displayProducts(arrayOfProducts));
```

A common pattern is to combine a flattening function with a mapping one, called flatMap. This type of function maps and *then* flattens, so the name's backward. Let's say you had a collection of friends who all had several favorite foods. We can use flatMap to create an array of all the foods you should serve at your next party:

```
let friends = [{
  name: 'Jill',
  favoriteFoods: ['pizza', 'hummus']
}, {
  name: 'Bob',
  favoriteFoods: ['ice cream']
}, {
  name: 'Alice',
  favoriteFoods: ['chicken wings', 'salmon']
}];

flatMap(friends, friend => friend.favoriteFoods);

// Step 1: map
[
  ['pizza', 'hummus'],
  ['ice cream'],
  ['chicken wings', 'salmon']
]
// Step 2: flatten (unwrapping each subarray)
['pizza', 'hummus', 'ice cream', 'chicken wings', 'salmon']
```

Unwrapping an *empty* array results in no data being passed on. This means you can use the flatMap function as a way to filter out results you're not interested in. Here, it's pulling out the data where it exists, and ignoring elements that errored:

```
let results = [
  { data: [1,2,3]},
  { error: 'Something went wrong'},
  { data: [7,5,7]},
  { data: [1,3,1]},
];

let dataPoints = flatMap(results, result => {
  if (result.data) {
    return result.data;
  }
  return [];
});

console.log(dataPoints); // [1,2,3,7,5,7,1,3,1]
```

While combining several sub-arrays into a single array is commonly known as *flattening*, in Rx-land combining multiple observables into a single observable is called *merging*. Think of this like several roads all merging into a single main road. Since flatMapping combines multiple observables into a single stream, the operator is called mergeMap.

Adding mergeMap to our example means replacing map(wordString => wordString. split(/\s+\)) with mergeMap(wordString => wordString.split(/\s+\)). This results in all following operators being called many times, each with a single word. This is in contrast to regular map where each operator only receives one event (an array containing the entire content of the textbox) per keystroke. This allows control of the granularity of a stream, which will become important when we dig into inner observables in the next section.

Reducing

Now that the array of words is being flattened into separate events, we need some way of handling each of these smaller, "inner" events. Effectively, two different streams of data are going on. One is the same stream from before: every keystroke triggers an event containing the current content of the textbox. The new stream is smaller (and finite), containing an event for every *word* in the textbox. Mixing these two would be problematic—the view rendering function wouldn't know whether a new word is a continuation of the inner stream, or represents the beginning of a new event from the original stream. There's no way to know when to clear the page without adding obtuse hacks to your code.

Instead of intermingling two different streams, we can create an *inner observable* to represent the stream of individual words. mergeMap makes this easy. If mergeMap's function returns an observable, mergeMap subscribes to it, so the programmer only needs to be concerned about the business logic. Any values emitted by the inner observable are then passed on to the outer observable. This inner observable neatly completes because there is a finite amount of data to process (unlike the event-based outer observable). The inner observable here uses the from constructor, which takes any unwrappable value (arrays, promises, other observables), unwraps that value, and passes each resulting item along as a separate event. Here, split returns an array, so the observable emits a new event for each string in the array.

```
mergeMap(wordString =>
  // Inner observable
  from(wordString.split(/\s+/))
  .pipe(
    map(pigLatinify),
    reduce((bigString, newWord) => bigString + ' ' + newWord, '')
  )
)
```

The inner observable is created using the from constructor, which takes an iterable, such as an array, and creates an observable containing all of the items in that iterable. In this instance, from passes on each word individually to the rest of the stream. The first operator is the same map we used before, passing each word to Pig Latin translation function. At the end of the inner observable is a new operator: reduce. Reduce works just like the regular JavaScript version does: given a collection of data, it applies a collection function to each item. When it's finished processing every item in the collection, it emits the final value down the stream (in this case, to the subscriber). It also takes a second argument—the initial value (an empty string).

> ### How reduce Works
>
> If you're unfamiliar with reduce, know that the central concept is that it takes a collection of values (like an array or observable stream) and reduces it to a single value. A reduce function takes two values: the accumulated value and the next value in the sequence. An array-based reducer to sum all of the numbers in an array looks like this:
>
> ```
> let total = [1, 2, 3].reduce((accumulatedValue, nextNumber)
>               => accumulatedValue + nextNumber);
> ```
>
> The reduce function also has an optional second parameter, which is the initial value of the accumulator. Otherwise, the first value of the array is used, so in the above example, the function is first called with 1 and 2 as arguments.

A simple reduce to sum all of the numbers in an observable stream looks a lot like the array example above (using an initial of value 0):

```
from([1,2,3])
.pipe(
  reduce((accumulator, val) => accumulator + val, 0)
)
.subscribe(console.log); // Logs `6` once
```

Debugging an Observable Stream

This inner observable keeps things simple when it comes to managing the split data, but it creates a bit of a mess in the middle of our previously-debuggable observable flow. Debugging was easy when there was only one observable—just add .subscribe(console.log) at the point of contention and comment out the rest. Now there are mutliple observable chains kicking around (and one of them doesn't even have an explicit subscribe). How can we peek into a running observable chain to see what's going on?

mapTo and mergeMapTo

Sometimes, we want to convert each element in a stream to a new value but don't really care about the current value of the event. Rx provides mapTo for just this purpose:

```
interval(1000)
.pipe(
  mapTo('Hello world!')
)
.subscribe(console.log); // logs 'Hello world!' every second
```

mergeMapTo also exists, allowing you to pass in any unwrappable item. Here, the button click event doesn't carry the information we want; all that matters is firing off a request to the logout endpoint. mapTo wouldn't work here, because it won't subscribe to the observable (which triggers the request):

```
fromEvent(myButton, 'click')
.pipe(
  mergeMapTo(ajax('/logout'))
)
.subscribe(console.log);
```

These two operators are most useful when the presence of an event in the stream signifies something's happened, but the event doesn't carry any useful information.

Enter the tap operator. This operator does not modify any of the in-flight data or observables surounding it. Instead, it allows us to peek into what's going on inside the stream, observing the data, but not manipulating it. This allows for debugging by logging or adding in other side effects (say, tracking application performance). Here, each value is logged twice, once from tap and once from subscribe. Run this yourself to confirm that tap is not manipulating the data, just passing it on:

```
interval(1000)
.pipe(
  tap(val => {
    console.log('inside tap', val);
    // This return doesn't change the final value
    return val * 100;
  })
)
.subscribe(val => console.log('inside subscribe', val));
```

In previous versions of RxJS, the tap operator was known as do. This changed in version 6 because do is a reserved word in Java-Script. Now that operators are imported as separate variables, it wouldn't *do* to have do as a variable. Instead, tap was used (and is more descriptive of what the operator does).

Here's the final version of the Pig Latin `mergeMap` example. Try adding a `tap` or two to inspect things at different points in the stream. Are the values what you'd expect?

vanilla/manipulatingStreams/pigLatin-complete.ts

```
import { fromEvent, from } from 'rxjs';
import { map, mergeMap, reduce } from 'rxjs/operators';

// Converts a word in English to one in Pig Latin
function pigLatinify(word) {
  // Handle single-letter case and empty strings
  if (word.length < 2) {
    return word;
  }
  return word.slice(1) + '-' + word[0] + 'ay';
}

fromEvent<any>(textbox, 'keyup')
.pipe(
  map(event => event.target.value),
  mergeMap(wordString =>
    // Inner observable
    from(wordString.split(/\s+/))
    .pipe(
      map(pigLatinify),
      reduce((bigString, newWord) => bigString + ' ' + newWord, '')
    )
  )
)
.subscribe(translatedWords => results.innerText = translatedWords);
```

In the case of Pig Latin, the array passed to the inner observable contains nothing more complicated than strings. We could get away without a `mergeMap` here. On the other hand, your observable chain might contain more complicated objects (as you'll see with the typeahead example). Using `mergeMap` to extract the contents of the array simplifies the operators that follow at the cost of adding a small amount of complexity in the form of an inner observable. As a general rule, if the contents of the array are complex (nested objects), or the per-item processing is complex (for instance, if there's async processing), it's best to use the `mergeMap` technique. Otherwise, the trade-off of added complexity through the inner observable isn't worth it.

Another debugging technique is the `toArray` operator, a specialized version of `reduce`. `toArray` waits for the stream to complete (which means it doesn't work with infinite streams), then emits all of the events in the stream as a single array. This is useful for debugging because it eliminates the asynchronous nature of a stream, so you can see the entire stream as a single collection. In this example, without take(3), the stream would never end, and toArray would never emit a value.

```
fromEvent(someButton, 'click')
.pipe(
  take(3),
  toArray()
)
.subscribe(console.log);
```

A third tool for debugging is the repeat operator, which does exactly what you think it does. When repeat is called on an observable, it waits for that observable to complete, then emits the values from the original observable however many times you specified. This example logs 1, 2, 3, 1, 2, 3, 1, 2, 3 (with each group of logs separated by one second).

```
of(1, 2, 3)
.pipe(
  delay(1000),
  repeat(3)
)
.subscribe(console.log);
```

When debugging short, finite streams, repeat is helpful to continue the stream so that you can dig into what's going on in your code (instead of refreshing the page every single time). It's important to note here that repeat(n) emits the source values n times, so repeat(1) behaves just like an unmodified observable. Calling repeat without an argument results in an infinite observable, repeating until unsubscribed.

Typeahead

Now that a Pig Latin translator is under your belt, let's tackle a different problem: typeahead. A typeahead system is one where, as the user types, the UI suggests possible options. In other words, the UI *types ahead* of the user. In the screenshot on page 28, typeahead helps to select a U.S. state. The user entered ar and the UI suggests all states that might fit ar, in alphabetical order.

There has been much gnashing of teeth and pulling of hair over typeaheads. Before observables, collecting the stream of keypress events and parsing out possible results was difficult to pull off and filled with with race conditions.

```
ar

  Arizona

  Arkansas

  Delaware

  Maryland

  North Carolina

  South Carolina
```

Don't just take my word for it; read through this imperative typeahead
implementation to see whether you can find the bug:

```
myInput.addEventListener('keyup', e => {
  let text = e.target.value;
  if (text.length < 2) { return; }
  let results = [];
  for (let i = 0; i < options.length; i++) {
    if (options[i].includes(text)) {
      results.push(options[i]);
    }
  }
  resultEl.innerHTML = '';
  for (let i = 0; i < results.length; i++) {
    resultEl.innerHTML += '<br>' + results;
  }
});
```

The deliberately inserted bug is in the last for loop. The code appends the
entire results array to resultEl several times, instead of each element being added
individually, which results in a conflagration of misparsed JSON, instead of
a nice, orderly list. This sort of bug is hard to find when reviewing imperative
code, because variables aren't isolated into single units of functionality.
Already there are problems with the imperative code, and we're not even
talking about asynchronous requests yet. Imagine how much more complicated
this code would get in a situation like Netflix, where the full database of
potential results is too big to store on the client side. Each keystroke would
trigger a new AJAX request. You'll figure out how to tackle that in *Advanced
Async*. For now, think about how you'd build something like this with Rx.

All done? Here's my implementation:

```
vanilla/manipulatingStreams/typeahead-complete.ts
import { fromEvent, from } from 'rxjs';
import { map, filter, tap, mergeMap, reduce} from 'rxjs/operators';

fromEvent<any>(typeaheadInput, 'keyup')
.pipe(
  map((e): string => e.target.value.toLowerCase()),
  tap(() => typeaheadContainer.innerHTML = ''),
  filter(val => val.length > 2),
  mergeMap(val =>
    from(usStates)
    .pipe(
      filter(state => state.includes(val)),
      map(state => state.split(val).join('<b>' + val + '</b>')),
      reduce((prev: any, state) => prev.concat(state), [])
    )
  )
)
.subscribe(
  (stateList: string[]) => typeaheadContainer.innerHTML += '<br>'
  + stateList.join('<br>')
);
```

The first line is familiar. Every keyup event emitted from the myInput element sends a new event object down the stream. The map operator takes that event object and plucks out the current *value* of the input (a string). This string is passed on to a new operator: filter. This operator works much like its namesake from arrays: It passes each datum into its function. If that function returns a truthy value, filter sends the datum down the line. If instead, the function returns a falsey value, filter does nothing—the value is not passed on. This filter in particular allows only values that are longer than two characters.

Now that the code is certain it has a value worth investigating, a tap operator clears the output element. Interacting with the web page is another way to use tap; at this point, the code does not care about *what* the value is, only that it was emitted. In these cases, tap is used to trigger a *side effect* (changing something outside of the immediate operator). In this case, the side effect clears the results area.

The final outer operator follows the mergeMap pattern above. The inner observable is made of the list of states (declared outside the snippet). Another filter selects only the states with a name that contains the current value of the input, using the ES6 includes operator. A map then bolds the instances of the current query, before a reduce collects them back into an observable. Finally, the subscribe call takes that list of states and adds them to the typeahead container element.

> ## The pluck Operator
>
> So far, one of the uses of map has been to pull out some property or properties of an object. In the previous example, the first map pulled the current value of the textbox from an event object. Rx provides the pluck operator for this common pattern. pluck takes one or more string arguments, which are the properties you wish to pluck off the object (in contrast to map taking a function).
>
> ```
> pluck('target', 'value')
> ```
>
> pluck has one more advantage over map: it's safe. If a property is missing, map will error out and kill the entire observable chain with: Cannot read property someProp of undefined. If pluck encounters the same situation, it just passes on undefined, keeping the observable flow healthy.

What We Learned

By now you've not only picked up some observable creation knowledge, but also added a whole host of operators to your skillset. In this chapter, you learned:

- How to flatten data with mergeMap
- How to filter out unwanted data with (unsurprisingly) filter
- How to collect an entire observable worth of data with reduce
- How to debug in-flight data with tap

You also tackled the concept of inner observables. By now you should start to see how observables can plug into common problems you face on the frontend. There's still plenty to go (two chapters would make a short book), but you've plowed through the basics. In the next chapter, you finally face the big dragon of asynchronicity. The challenge ramps up, but I think you can handle it. See you there!

CHAPTER 3

Managing Asynchronous Events

If you're anything like me, at some point you've played a video game. And if you've played a video game, you've been frustrated at how long it takes things to load. A long time ago, I waited patiently for a game to load on our 56k connection, not realizing that something had failed and the loading bar's status would be stuck at 99% for all eternity. Many years later, I'm getting my revenge by griping about it in a programming book. Right, back on topic.

At this point in your RxJS journey, you may feel like that old Wendy's commercial: "Sure, Pig Latin was fun, but where's the beef?" This is the beef chapter you've been waiting for. You'll dive into asynchronous programming on top of RxJS and never look at an AJAX call the same way again. So much of frontend coding is tied up in handling multiple AJAX calls around the internet.

Until this chapter, RxJS has been merely convienent. In this chapter, you'll build a progress bar. OK, progress bars aren't terribly exciting, but there's a lot wrapped up in there. Your attitude toward RxJS will shift from "convenient" to "indispensible" after you see how well RxJS handles multiple asynchronous requests flying around without breaking a sweat. Along the way, you'll learn about making AJAX requests with Rx, error handling, a swath of new operators, and advanced uses of subscribe.

Making AJAX Requests

ajax is another helper constructor; this one performs an AJAX request. It returns an observable of a single value: whatever the AJAX request returns. Here's a simple example (note that the ajax constructor is imported from a different location than the other constructors):

```
import { ajax } from 'rxjs/ajax';

ajax('/api/managingAsync/ajaxExample')
.subscribe(console.log);
```

Running this code *does not* log data about the AJAX request to the console. Instead, a big fat error message appears in the console informing us that the URL I told you to request doesn't exist. Until now you've only encountered well-behaved observables that never throw errors. Now that your code is making network requests, it's time to figure out how to deal with unexpected problems.

Handling Errors

As powerful as observables are, they can't prevent errors from happening. Instead, they provide a concrete way to gracefully handle errors as they arise. Errors are handled in the subscribe call (same as regular data). So far, the examples have only passed a single parameter to .subscribe—a function that runs for every datum that arrives at the end of the stream. Turns out, a total of *three* parameters can be passed in (the latter two being optional):

```
.subscribe(
  function next(val) { /* A new value has arrived */ },
  function error(err) { /* An error occured */ },
  function done() { /* The observable is done */ }
);
```

The first (the one you've been using until this point) is known as the next function. It's called on every new value passed down the observable—this is the option you've been using. The second, error, is called when an error occurs at some point in the observable stream. Once an error happens, no further data is sent down the observable and the root unsubscribe functions are called. The observable is considered to be in an "error" state (much like promises) and needs to be resubscribed to get any more data (later in this chapter, you'll learn how to do that with the retry operator). Finally, the done function is called when the observable finishes. Not all observables will finish—fromEvent is an example of such an *infinite* observable. For *finite* observables (like the inner observable created in *Manipulating Streams*), done is an important thing to know about. While it's possible to handle all three cases by passing in each function as a separate argument to subscribe, the following single-argument example is also valid:

```
.subscribe({
  next: val => { /* A new value has arrived */},
  err: err => { /* An error occured */},
  done: () => { /* The observable is done */}
});
```

As we covered in *Creating Observables*, you'll notice that this object also qualifies as an observer. Any valid observer can be passed directly into .subscribe. Technically, none of the properties are mandatory. If you had a large pile of data to process but only cared that the processing was done, you could pass in an object with only the done property. Strictly speaking, it's valid to pass an empty object to .subscribe, but it's not very useful. When you reach *Multiplexing Observables*, you'll find some advanced RxJS classes, which are observers in addition to being observables.

Most of the time engineers just use the simpler non-observer version unless there's a reason to skip the next or error functions, such as when a function needs to send a value to a server, but doesn't care about the return data.

Now, let's go back to that earlier AJAX example and add some error handling.

```
ajax('/api/managingAsync/ajaxExample')
.subscribe(
  result => console.log(result),
  err => alert(err.message)
);
```

Now that a clear error message is presented, we can diagnose the problem immediately—the route that is being requested does not exist. If this was a user-facing page, you could use the error handler to display relevant information to the user. In this case, it's a quick fix to update the URL the request is sent to:

```
ajax('/api/managingAsync/correctAjaxExample')
.subscribe(
  result => console.log(result),
  err => alert(err.message)
);
```

Throwing Your Own Errors

Sometimes things just won't work out, and you need to throw an error manually. RxJS provides the throwError constructor to an observable stream that immediately enters the error state:

```
throwError(new Error('Augh!'))
.subscribe({
  next: () => console.log('This will never be called'),
  error: err => console.error('This is immediately called', err)
});
```

The throwError constructor is particularly useful when testing your website to ensure errors are handled properly and bubble up useful information to the user.

Promises vs. Observables with AJAX

A question that always comes up when discussing using observables to make AJAX requests is: "Why not promises?" As we learned in *Creating Observables*, a promise represents a *single* value delivered over time where an observable represents *multiple* values. An AJAX request is a single value—why complicate things?

Promises are simpler in concept, but the real world always complicates things. Pretend you're developing the mobile platform for a ridesharing app. Users will typically use the app outside, away from solid Wi-Fi. They're trying to get somewhere, so they have a low tolerance for latency and errors. With that in mind, we'll use the following code to build the best user experience for updating the user on the status of their ride:

```
let request$ = interval(5000)
.pipe(
  mergeMap(() =>
    ajax('/carStatus.json')
    .pipe(retry(3))
  )
);

let carStatus = request$.subscribe(updateMap, displayError);

// Later, when the car arrives
carStatus.unsubscribe();
```

This observable stream starts off using the interval constructor from *Creating Observables*, triggering every five seconds. mergeMap is used to handle an inner observable that makes a request to the backend for the latest update on the car's status. This is a twist on the mergeMap pattern you've seen before—mergeMap works as usual, but the inner observable makes an AJAX request instead. Piped through the inner AJAX observable is an operator you haven't seen before: retry(3). Intuitively, this operator retries the source observable when an error occurs. Mechanically, this means that on an error, it unsubscribes from the source observable (cleaning everything up from the original request) and then resubscribes (triggering the constructor logic, and therefore the AJAX request again). This retry means that in the event of a shaky connection dropping the request, the request will be made up to three times before finally giving up, resulting in a much better user experience. Finally, we subscribe, updating the map every time a request successfully goes through. If all three requests fail, an error is shown to the user—possibly, they're out of signal range.

This example shows that observables can be used for much smarter error handling and for better user experience without sacrificing code simplicity.

Joe asks:
Can I Use Observables with Promises?

Many APIs prefer the simplicity of promises over the power of observables. Fortunately, RxJS integrates easily with promise-based systems with the constructor fromPromise and operator toPromise. The constructor takes a promise and emits whatever the promise resolves to, completing the observable immediately after. In this example, we take the native fetch API and wrap it in an observable:

```
function fetchObservable(endpoint) {
  let requestP = fetch(endpoint)
  .then(res => res.json());
  return fromPromise(requestP);
}

fetchObservable('/user')
.subscribe(console.log);
```

On the other hand, perhaps you're working with a library that expects you to pass in a promise. In that case, the operator toPromise will save your bacon. It waits for the observable to complete and then resolves the promise with the collection of all data the observable emitted. This operator is particularly helpful when refactoring an old, promise-based architecture to use observables:

```
let helloP = of('Hello world!')
.toPromise();

helloP.then(console.log);
```

Sometimes fromPromise isn't needed at all. Many RxJS constructors and operators that take an observable will also take a promise and do the conversion for you at the library level. The Car Status example can be adapted to use the fetch API, though some of the advantages of RxJS are lost (in this example, easy access to 'retry').

```
let request$ = interval(5000)
.pipe(
  mergeMap(() =>
    fetch('/carStatus.json')
    .then(res => res.json())
  )
);

let carStatus = request$.subscribe(updateMap, displayError);

// Later, when the car arrives
carStatus.unsubscribe();
```

While it may be tempting to switch between observables and promises whenever one is more convenient, I recommend that you stick to the same abstraction whenever possible. This will keep your codebase more consistent and reduce surprises down the road.

When we're at our desks, making requests to a server running on our machine, things rarely go wrong. Out in the field, *everything* can and will go wrong. An AJAX request is *conceptually* a single value, but there's a lot to be gained from treating one as a potential source of failure (and therefore multiple values). Observables let us gracefully retry when things go wrong. In the next section, you'll learn how to deal with failure when retrying isn't an option.

Loading with Progress Bar

That was the theory—now to build something practical. If you've ever implemented a loading bar that pulled together many different bits, you know just how irritating it can be to wrangle all those requests together. Common pre-observable asynchronous patterns plan for only one listener for each event. This results in ridiculous loading bar hacks, like adding a function call to every load event or monkey patching XMLHttpRequest. Using RxJS, our software never leaves our users waiting at 99% (not that I'm bitter).

 In the following example, the progress bar represents mutiple requests. It's also possible to use the same strategies to represent a single large request by listening in to the progress event of an XMLHttpRequest.

Let's start out with 100 requests from the ajax constructor, all collected together in an array. Load up vanilla/managingAsync/mosaic.ts and code along.

```
vanilla/managingAsync/mosaic-complete.ts
let requests = [];
for (let x = 0; x < 10; x++) {
  for (let y = 0; y < 10; y++) {
    let endpoint =
      `http://localhost:3000/api/managingAsync/assets/coverpart-${x}-${y}.png`;
    let request$ = ajax({
      url: endpoint,
      responseType: 'blob'
    })
    .pipe(
      map(res => ({
        blob: res.response,
        x,
        y
      }))
    );
    requests.push(request$);
  }
}
```

At any time, there will always be a large number of requests to track, even in a singleplayer game. In *Reactive Game Development*, you'll build out an entire game based on a RxJS backbone. For now you'll just build the loading bar. (If it feels a bit strange to build the loading bar before the game, remember that this is a chance to catch unexpected bugs.) To track the overall state of the game load, all of these AJAX observables need to be combined into a single observable. There's a merge constructor that takes any number of parameters (as long as they're all observables) and returns a single observable that will emit a value whenever any of the source observables emit. This example uses ES6's spread operator to transform the array into a series of individual parameters:

vanilla/managingAsync/mosaic-complete.ts
```
merge(...requests)
.subscribe(
  val => drawToPage(val),
  err => alert(err)
);
```

This single subscribe to the merged observables kicks off all of the requests in one fell swoop. Every request is centrally handled, and the user is notified when something goes wrong. Write out this example in mosaic.js and refresh the page.

If everything worked, the image comes together on the page as each individual request is loaded as shown in the screenshot on page 38.

The Two Merges

In the above example, merge is used as a *constructor* (a way to create a new observable). However, it's also an *operator*:

```
let obsOne$ = interval(1000);
let obsTwo$ = interval(1500);

// Piping through the merge operator
obsOne$
.pipe(
  merge(obsTwo$)
)
.subscribe(console.log);

// Is the same as using the merge constructor

merge(obsOne$, obsTwo$)
.subscribe(console.log);
```

In cases where everything starts at the same time (like the loading bar), merge used as a constructor is simpler than the operator form. The operator form of merge comes in handy when you're in the middle of an observable chain and want to add in more data.

In this particular example, the tiles of the mosaic provide an abstract loading bar. In the auteur video game designer life, there are no such affordances. To build an award-winning game, the loading bar needs to be notified as each request completes. Previously, the reduce operator collected each item and only emitted the resulting collection after the original observable *completed*. Instead, we want the data collecting ability of reduce, but we want the operator to emit the latest value on every new item. Digging deeper into the RxJS toolbox, you find scan. scan is an impatient reduce. Instead of politely waiting for the orignal stream to complete, scan blurts out the latest result on every event.

Here's scan in action, tracking how many requests have finished and emitting the total percentage on every event (arrayOfRequests is declared outside this snippet, see the loading-complete.ts file for the full details):

```
vanilla/managingAsync/loading-complete.ts
import { merge } from 'rxjs';
import { scan } from 'rxjs/operators';

merge(...arrayOfRequests)
.pipe(
  scan((prev) => prev + (100 / arrayOfRequests.length), 0)
)
.subscribe(percentDone => {
  progressBar.style.width = percentDone + '%';
  progressBar.innerText = Math.round(percentDone) + '%';
});
```

Like reduce, scan has two parameters: a reducer function and an initial value. scan's function also takes two values—the current internal state and the latest item to be passed down the stream. This example throws away the latest value, because the loading bar doesn't care about *what* information came back, just that it *successfully* came back. scan then increments the internal counter by one unit (a unit is defined as 100 divided by the number of requests, so this results in the percent of the total that each request represents). If you've been lucky, you haven't hit any errors so far. Time to change that.

When Good AJAX Goes Bad

I've prepared a slightly different observable for you in errors.js. This new observable still has all the requests, but they hit a different endpoint on the node server. This new endpoint is programmed to give up and start spitting errors after several dozen requests. Using your knowledge from earlier in the chapter, pass in a function to handle the case where some requests fail to complete.

```
vanilla/managingAsync/errors-complete.ts
loadingRequestsBad$
.pipe(
  scan((prev) => prev + (100 / arrayOfRequests.length), 0)
)
.subscribe(percentDone => {
  progressBar.style.width = percentDone + '%';
  progressBar.innerText = Math.round(percentDone) + '%';
}, err => {
  console.log(err);
  msgArea.innerText = 'Something went wrong, please try again';
  msgArea.style.display = 'block';
});
```

Aha! Now when the server falls over, it's gracefully handled—the user is informed that something's gone wrong and has some basic remediation instructions. You've built an app that can survive even the harshest of conditions without skipping a beat. Users may vent on Twitter, but at least they'll be venting about the right thing.

Not Doing Everything at Once

In this case, a single subscribe launched 128 AJAX requests. In a browser environment, the number of concurrent AJAX requests to the same domain is limited. In other environments (say, a quick Node script), you may have a long list of tasks and want to limit how many can run at once. The merge constructor and operator include an optional parameter to do just that. Pass in a number as the final argument, and merge will only subscribe to that number of observables at once. Just be careful you don't have any infinite streams in there!

```
// Will only run five requests at a time
merge(...arrayOfRequests, 5)
.pipe(
  scan((prev, val) => prev + (100 / arrayOfRequests.length), 0)
)
.subscribe(updateProgressbar, handleError);
```

Progressive and Ordered Loading

The previous snippet assumes the game is made up of 128 separate items, all of the same priority. If the game includes a main UI, as well as separate sections for chat, the player's inventory, and a market for players to exchange items, the player needs to wait for *everything* to load, even if they don't care about today's prices for Fizzblonium. The next step is to break up the game into *components*. Each section of functionality (UI, inventory, chat, market) will have all of the parts required for operation in its own load observable.

This way, each component of the game interface can decide what needs to be loaded for that component. Additionally, this would let us control the order that the app's component parts load in. Taking the same progress bar pattern as before:

```
merge(...componentRequestArray, 5)
.pipe(
  scan((prev, val) => prev + (100 / componentRequestArray.length), 0)
)
.subscribe(updateProgressbar, handleError);
```

Unfortunately, we need to trigger our three subcomponents when the main load has *finished*, not just when there's a new value. Right now, the only option is to pile all the things into an if statement in the the initial subscribe.

```
merge(...componentRequestArray, 5)
.pipe(
  scan((prev, val) => prev + (100 / componentRequestArray.length), 0)
)
.subscribe(percentDone => {
  if (percentDone === 100) {
    // Trigger the other observables
    marketLoader$.subscribe();
    chatLoader$.subscribe();
    inventoryLoader$.subscribe();
  }
  updateProgressbar(percentDone);
}, handleError);
```

This is starting to get ugly. And everything constantly resets on every game load. A player may not care about the market and want it closed. We can save the user's state and load it, at the cost of further complicating the subscribe function:

```
merge(...componentRequestArray, 5)
.pipe(
  scan((prev, val) => prev + (100 / componentRequestArray.length), 0)
)
.subscribe(percentDone => {
  if (percentDone === 100) {
    ajax('/userPreferences')
    .subscribe(results => {
      // Trigger the other observables
      if (results.marketOpen) {
        marketLoader$.subscribe();
      }
      if (results.chatOpen) {
        chatLoader$.subscribe();
      }
      if (results.inventoryOpen) {
        inventoryLoader$.subscribe();
      }
    }, handleError);
  }
  updateProgressbar(percentDone);
}, handleError);
```

Yikes, this is getting pretty complicated. The whole point of using RxJS is it allows us to move each action into a single function. This code is starting to resemble all of the terrible patterns from the callback world. There's a problem with the observables you've used so far—they're single-use only, with new subscriptions creating entirely new streams. If we could take a single stream and split it to multiple subscribers, things like this would get a lot simpler. We'll cover the exact mechanics of "observable splitting" in *Multiplexing Observables*.

What We Learned

Observables are at their best when you're dealing with asynchronous events. You've learned how to make AJAX requests to an external server, how to batch together requests, and how to handle errors when they occur. We also peeked into a larger world of multiple layers of loading.

In the next chapter, you'll progress to more advanced AJAX topics: avoiding race conditions and playing nice with external APIs.

CHAPTER 4

Advanced Async

BANG! The starting gun goes off as two functions shoot down the track. Firing off AJAX requests willy-nilly, the competing functions zip around corner after corner until finally, one reaches the finish line inches before the other. The functions line up in the winner's circle as the judge pulls out the envelope. Suddenly, pandemonium erupts when the envelope reveals that the functions weren't supposed to finish in that order! Disaster!

Fortunately, software development isn't that exciting (I don't think I could deal with that every day). Still, functions finishing in the wrong order can spell disaster. In this chapter, you learn how clever Rx use can prevent race conditions before they have a chance to happen. The previous chapters covered areas where observables are helpful, but not transformative. Now you'll build something where Rx completely changes the development cycle: a typeahead module that makes an AJAX request to grab results.

The Spec

You're putting on the hat of a programmer who works at StackOverflow. Management has decreed that the old search box is uncool and not Web 2.0 enough. You are to build a search box that *automatically searches for the user* without them needing to press the Enter key. In addition, you'll need to avoid overloading the backend servers. This means the code needs to prevent unnecessary requests.

Preventing Race Conditions with switchMap

In the Days of Olde, when magic still roamed the land, a High Programmer insulted a Network, and ever since then, the networks have had it out for us programmers. A typeahead race condition bug typically manifests itself like so:

1. user types a

2. get/render response for a

3. user types ab

4. user types abc

5. get/render response for abc

6. get/render response for ab

This could happen for many reasons—an ISP could have directed the abc query through a less-congested router, abc could have had fewer possible answers, resulting in a faster query, or the Network remembered that grudge from a long time ago. Regardless of the reason, our user now has the wrong results in front of them. How can you prevent this terrible tragedy?

Back in the days of VanillaJS, a solution might have started off based on an event listener:

```
let latestQuery;
searchBar.addEventListener('keyup', event => {
  let searchVal = latestQuery = event.target.value;
  fetch(endpoint + searchVal)
  .then(results => {
    if (searchVal === latestQuery) {
      updatePage(results);
    }
  });
});
```

Technically, this works though the exterior variable latestQuery might lead to some raised eyebrows in a code review. Look at this observable solution:

```
fromEvent(searchBar, 'keyup')
.pipe(
  pluck('target', 'value'),
  switchMap(query => ajax(endpoint + searchVal))
)
.subscribe(results => updatePage(results));
```

As usual, a new operator has snuck in for you to learn. This time it's switchMap—an operator that's been stealing notes from mergeMap. switchMap works the same way as mergeMap: for every item, it runs the inner observable, waiting for it to complete before sending the results downstream. There's one big exception: if a new value arrives *before the inner observable initiated by the previous value completes,* switchMap unsubscribes from the observable request (therefore cancelling it) and fires off a new one. This means that you can implement custom unsubscribe logic for your own observables (like the ones you built in *Creating Observables*).

In the switchMap example above, abc would be passed to switchMap before the query for ab is finished, and therefore, ab's result would be thrown away with nary a care. One way to think about this is that switchMap *switches* to the new request. The Rx version of the typeahead has each step wrapped up in its own functional package, leading to much more organized code. Let's look at what happens now when the network requests get mixed up:

1. user types a

2. switchMap sees a, makes a note

3. get/render response for a

4. switchMap removes note for a

5. user types ab

6. switchMap sees ab, makes a note

7. user types abc

8. switchMap sees abc, sees that it has a note about ab

9. switchMap *replaces* the ab note with one about abc

10. get/render response for abc

11. switchMap removes note for abc

12. get response for ab

13. switchMap sees response for ab and discards it because there's no corresponding note

That's a lot going on behind the scenes! Thankfully, the RxJS library handles all of these details.

Both the addEventListener and fromEvent snippets are missing part of the requirements—they don't wait for the user to stop typing before making a request, leading to a lot of unneeded requests. This is a great way to make the backend engineers angry—let's avoid that. Instead, how about you implement a debounce function?

Debouncing Events

There comes a time when several events fire in a row, and we don't want to do something on every event, but rather, when the events *stop* firing for a specified period. In the typeahead case, we only want to make requests when the user stops typing. A function set up in this way is known as a *debounced* function. To create such a debounced function, you pass a function into debounce, which then returns another function that wraps the original function:

```
let logPause = () => console.log('There was a pause in the typing');
// This won't work, it will log on every keystroke
// input.addEventListener('keydown', logPause);
// Instead, we debounce logPause
let logPauseDebounced = debounce(logPause);
input.addEventListener('keydown', logPauseDebounced);
```

You can even write your own helper to wrap a regular function into a debounced function:

vanilla/advancedAsync/debounce.js
```
function debounce(fn, delay=333) {
  let time;
  return function (...args) {
    if (time) {
      clearTimeout(time);
    }
    time = setTimeout(() => fn(...args), delay);
  }
}
```

 Choosing a duration to wait in a debounce is more of an art than a science. A default of 333 ms usually works when waiting for a user to stop typing.

Debounce can be a bit confusing at first. Let's put our debounce function through an example and watch what goes on:

vanilla/advancedAsync/debounce.js
```
let f = debounce((num) => console.log('debounced!  Arg:', num));

// Call synchronously
f(1);
f(2);
f(3);
f(4);
f(5);

// Call several times in a short interval
let i = 0;
let interval = setInterval(() => {
  console.log(++i);
  f(i);
}, 100);

setTimeout(() => clearInterval(interval), 1000);
```

Throttling Events

Sometimes a debounce is more complicated than what you really need. The throttle operator acts as a time-based filter. After it allows a value through, it won't allow a new value, until a preset amount of time has passed. All other values are thrown away. This can be useful when you connect to a noisy websocket that sends a lot more data than you need. For instance, you might be building a dashboard to keep the ops folks informed about all of their systems, and the monitoring backend sends updates on CPU usage several dozen times a second. DOM updates are slow, and that level of granularity isn't helpful anyway. Here, we just update the page every half-second.

```
cpuStatusWebsocket$
.pipe(throttle(500))
.subscribe(cpuVal => {
  cpuPercentElement.innerText = cpuVal;
});
```

debounce wouldn't work in this scenario; it would be left eternally waiting for a time when there is a pause in the updates around CPU usage. In the typeahead case, we do want to wait for a pause in activity, so we'll use debounce instead of throttle.

Adding Debounce to the Typeahead

One of the ways to determine the quality of code is to see how resilient the code is to change.

Let's see how the vanilla snippet fares when adding debouncing:

```
let latestQuery;
searchBar.addEventListener('keyup', debounce(event => {
  let searchVal = latestQuery = event.target.value;
  fetch(endpoint + searchVal)
  .then(results => {
    if (searchVal === latestQuery) {
      updatePage(results);
    }
  });
}));
```

Not much of a change, though it's easy to miss the fact that the event function is debounced, which may lead to confusion if someone inherits the project. One could extract the inner function into a separate variable, adding more code but enhancing clarity. On the other hand, how does the Rx version do?

```
fromEvent(searchBar, 'keyup')
.pipe(
  pluck('target', 'value'),
  debounceTime(333),
  switchMap(query => ajax(endpoint + searchVal))
)
.subscribe(results => updatePage(results));
```

Only one line is added, and where the debounce fits is clear to everyone who reads the code. Specifically, this is the debounceTime operator, which works along the lines of the debounce function written in the previous snippet—it waits until there's a 333 ms gap between events and then emits the most recent event, ignoring the rest. If another developer wants to change where the debounce happens or the length of the debounce, it's obvious how that change is accomplished.

Code quality is often a subjective metric, but you can already see how organized code becomes with RxJS. Everything is written in the order it's executed. Variables are declared close to where they're used (often on the same line), guarding against a whole category of scoping bugs. Each unit of functionality is encapsulated in its own function, without cross-cutting concerns. For the rest of this example, we'll drop the vanilla JavaScript and just use RxJS. This is, after all, a book about RxJS.

Skipping Irrelevant Requests

Now that the typeahead has debounceTime plugged in, far fewer requests are sent. That said, a lot of requests are still being sent, so there's work yet to do. You have two more tricks up your sleeve to cut down on these superfluous requests. The first is filter (you'll recall from *Manipulating Streams*), which you can use to remove items that won't provide useful results. Requests of three or fewer characters aren't likely to provide relevant information (a list of all the StackOverflow questions that include the letter a isn't terribly helpful), so filter allows searches only where the query has more than three characters:

```
fromEvent(searchBar, 'keyup')
.pipe(
  pluck('target', 'value'),
  filter(query => query.length > 3),
  debounceTime(333),
  switchMap(query => ajax(endpoint + searchVal))
)
.subscribe(results => updatePage(results));
```

So far, so good. This code only makes a request when the user stops typing, and there's a detailed enough query to be useful. There's one last optimization to make: keyup will fire on *any* keystroke, not just one that modifies the query (such as the left and right arrow keys). In this case, making a request with an identical query isn't useful, so you want to dispose of any identical events until there's a new query. Unlike the generic filter operator that looks at only one value at a time, this is a *temporal* filter. Some state handling is involved, since this new filter needs to compare each value to a previously-stored one. Instead of dealing with the messy state handling ourselves, Rx provides the distinctUntilChanged operator. distinctUntilChanged works just how you want it to—it keeps track of the last value to be passed along, and only passes on a new value when it is *different* from the previous value. You can add this in with a single line and head out for an early lunch.

```
fromEvent(searchBar, 'keyup')
.pipe(
  pluck('target', 'value'),
  filter(query => query.length > 3),
  distinctUntilChanged(),
  debounceTime(333),
  switchMap(query => ajax(endpoint + searchVal))
)
.subscribe(results => updatePage(results));
```

Handling Response Data

Right now, a single function (updatePage) is handling all the results. There's also no error handling. Quick, add an error handler using the techniques you learned in *Managing Asynchronous Events*:

```
fromEvent(searchBar, 'keyup')
.pipe(
  pluck('target', 'value'),
  filter(query => query.length > 3),
  distinctUntilChanged(),
  debounceTime(333),
  switchMap(query => ajax(endpoint + searchVal))
)
.subscribe(
  results => updatePage(results),
  err => handleErr(err)
);
```

This error handler handles the error gracefully and unsubscribes from the stream. When your observable enters the errored state, it no longer detects keystrokes, and the typeahead stops working. We need some way to handle errors without entering the error state. The catchError operator does just that.

Using catchError

The catchError operator is simple on the surface—it triggers whenever an error is thrown, but it provides plenty of options for how you handle the next steps. catchError takes two parameters: the error that was thrown and the current observable that's being run. If all we cared about in an error state was that an error was thrown, we could write the catchError operator like this:

```
catchError(err => {
  throw err;
})
```

This catchError function acts as if it had never been included in the first place. For the use of catchError to make sense, one common use case is to throw a new, more descriptive error:

```
catchError(err => {
  throw 'Trouble getting predictions from the server';
})
```

This still results in the observable entering the errored state, but the error is clear. Now, what if we want to continue on instead of entering the errored state? We need to tap into the second parameter passed to catchError—the observable itself. This is tricky to conceptualize, so let's start with the code:

```
catchError((err, caught$) => {
  return caught$;
})
```

If the catchError operator doesn't throw a new error, Rx takes a look at what it has returned. Rx looks for anything that can be easily turned into an observable; an array, a promise, or another observable are all valid options. Rx then converts the return value into an observable (if needed), and now the rest of the observable chain can subscribe to the new, returned observable. If all catchError does is return the original observable, the rest of the chain continues unabated.

However, we don't want to completely ignore errors—it'd be nice if we could note the error somehow without completely breaking the typeahead. In other words, we want to return a new observable that contains both an object with error information as well as the original observable. This is the perfect case for the merge operator you learned about in *Managing Asynchronous Events*.

```
catchError((err, caught$) => {
  return merge(of({err}), caught$);
})
```

In the typeahead, we add catchError right after the switchMap, so it can catch any AJAX errors. We want the typeahead to keep working even when things go wrong, so we borrow the merge pattern.

```
fromEvent(searchBar, 'keyup')
.pipe(
  pluck('target', 'value'),
  filter(query => query.length > 3),
  distinctUntilChanged(),
  debounceTime(333),
  switchMap(query => ajax(endpoint + searchVal)),
  catchError((err, caught$) =>
    merge(of({err}), caught$)
  )
)
.subscribe(function updatePageOrErr(results) {
  if (results.err) {
    displayErr(results.err);
  } else {
    displayResults(results.data);
  }
});
```

Notice that the function passed into subscribe has also changed. updatePageOrErr is smart enough to check whether the err property exists on results and display a handy error message instead of the results. Semantically speaking, this is a bit confusing—the code now treats an error like any other value. At this point, it's better to think of an event as an update, rather than always containing new data for the typeahead. However, this allows our UI to be informative (errors are happening) without dying on the first error.

One finishing touch—let's show off a bit and add a loading spinner. We know something's actually changed when a value hits the switchMap, so just before the switchMap, add a tap operator that will display the loading spinner. Another tap just after the catch (or when the request has completed) will hide the spinner. These tap operations let us isolate side effects from the main business logic:

```
vanilla/advancedAsync/searchbar-complete.ts
fromEvent<any>(searchBar, 'keyup')
.pipe(
  map(event => event.target.value),
  filter(query => query.length > 3),
  distinctUntilChanged(),
  debounceTime(333),
  tap(() => loadingEl.style.display = 'block'),
  switchMap(query => ajax(endpoint + query)),
```

```
      catchError((err, caught$) =>
        merge(of({ err }), caught$)
      ),
      tap(() => loadingEl.style.display = 'none')
)
.subscribe(function updatePageOrErr(results: any) {
      if (results.err) {
        alert(results.err);
      } else {
        displayResults(results.response);
      }
    },
    err => alert(err.message)
);
```

Building a Stock Ticker

In the previous section, we built a typeahead. That covered only one kind of asynchronous flow—the frontend always triggers the initiating event and then waits for a response. The backend never provides new data unless the frontend specifically asks for it.

In this section, you're going to build a stock market viewer, which will display the (randomly-generated) prices of several fake stocks in real time. The server will send data to the frontend at any time, and the code needs to be ready to react to new events. In additon, the Rx stream needs to track the current state of each stock ticker for display on the page. As a cherry on top to let you really flex your Rx muscles, we'll add some on-page filters that require their own streams.

This is your biggest challenge yet. The first thing to write is the constructor. A constructor that's specifically for websockets is built into RxJS:

vanilla/advancedAsync/stocks-complete.ts
```
let endpoint = 'ws://localhost:3000/api/advancedAsync/stock-ws';
// No semicolon at the end here - this is continued in the next snippet
let stockStream$ = webSocket(endpoint)
```

Subjects

 stockStream$ isn't a standard observable like you've seen so far—rather, it's a Subject, an object that's a turbocharged observable. For the purposes of this section, stockStream$ acts just like a regular observable. In *Multiplexing Observables*, you'll learn about the other neat tricks subjects have up their sleeves.

So the graph can render the stock's value changes over time, next we need to record the last ten values this observable emitted. When a stream wants to *accumulate* values, you'd turn to reduce or scan. In this case, we want to use scan, because it emits a new value for every event on the stream, whereas reduce waits for the stream to complete. This stream never ends, so we use scan.

We can also use scan to accumulate a limited number of values by adding a check for total length of the array. (You need to adjust the data from time-based buckets into stock-based buckets with an extra map.)

vanilla/advancedAsync/stocks-complete.ts
```
.pipe(
  scan((accumulatedData, nextItem) => {
    accumulatedData.push(nextItem);
    if (accumulatedData.length > 10) {
      // Remove the frontmost (i.e. oldest) item
      accumulatedData.shift();
    }
    return accumulatedData;
  }, []), // Remember, the second parameter to `scan` is the initial state
  map(newDataSet => {
    let intermediary = newDataSet.reduce((prev, datum) => {
      datum.forEach(d => {
        if (!prev[d.label]) {
          prev[d.label] = []
        }
        prev[d.label].push(d.price);
      })
      return prev;
    }, {});
    return Object.keys(intermediary).map(key => {
      // convert into something chart.js can read
      return {
        label: key,
        data: intermediary[key],
        fill: false,
        backgroundColor: colorMap[key],
        borderColor: colorMap[key]
      }
    });
  })
)
```

Couple that with a subscribe call that updates the graph on the page with new data and tells it to rerender, and you have a live-updating graph:

vanilla/advancedAsync/stocks-complete.ts
```
.subscribe(newDataSet => {
  config.data.datasets = newDataSet;
  stockChart.update();
}, err => console.error(err));
```

You now have a nice graph on the page, which automatically updates with the latest data from the websocket. The frontend only needed to open up the initial connection and then listen in for any further information. The next step is to add some interactivity to the page, to allow the user to filter down and look at only the stock details they're interested in.

Live Filtering the Stream

At this point, the stock graph shows four different stocks. We want to make the display of each stock configurable, which requires a live filter—we can't write a static one and call it a day. One solution is to simply recreate the entire observable stream on every click—a complicated method that also has the consequence of eliminating any data we've already cached. Instead, we opt for a series of merges that, while still complicated, allow dynamic filtering of all values on the graph without losing any in-flight data.

First, we need an observable of all updates to the stock filter. Notice four checkboxes on the side of the graph, one for each stock to filter. We need to listen in to each one, and map to the latest value, along with a signifier that indicates what stock is attached to that new value. After we have four streams, we need to combine them into the main websocket stream so that the render function for the graph can label the values correctly.

The first task is a review for you—the fromEvent constructor and a pair of map operators give us a stream of the latest check box state coupled with the stock tag it represents.

```
fromEvent(abcCheck, 'check')
.pipe(
  map(e => e.target.value),
  map(val => ({
    val,
    stock: 'abc'
  }))
)
```

However, we'd need to write (or more realistically, copy/paste) this snippet four times to get the four checkbox streams. Instead, let's abstract the stream creation into a function (and prime the pump with some initial data while we're at it):

```
function makeCheckboxStream(checkboxEl, stockName) {
  return merge(
    fromEvent(checkboxEl, 'change'),
    // Start off checked
    of({ target: { checked: true }})
  )
  .pipe(
    map(e => e.target.checked),
    map(isEnabled => ({
      isEnabled,
      stock: stockName
    }))
  );
}
```

The next step is to group these four observables together. As you learned
before, one option is to use the merge constructor:

```
merge(
  makeCheckboxStream(abcEl, 'abc'),
  makeCheckboxStream(defEl, 'def'),
  makeCheckboxStream(ghiEl, 'ghi'),
  makeCheckboxStream(jklEl, 'jkl')
)
```

The merge constructor does only half the job here. Though it combines the
streams, we still need to store the latest value from each stream somewhere.
Let's use the combineLatest constructor. combineLatest takes any number of
observables and returns a single stream, just like merge. The difference is that
combineLatest tracks the latest value of each input observable, and when any
of them emits a value, combineLatest emits an array containing the latest values
from each observable.

```
combineLatest(
  makeCheckboxStream(abcEl, 'abc'),
  makeCheckboxStream(defEl, 'def'),
  makeCheckboxStream(ghiEl, 'ghi'),
  makeCheckboxStream(jklEl, 'jkl')
)
.subscribe(console.log);
```

With the previous stream setup, every change results in the following being
logged to the console (with the isEnabled values tracking the checkboxes):

```
[{
  isEnabled: true,
  stock: 'abc'
}, {
  isEnabled: true,
  stock: 'def'
}, {
  isEnabled: true,
  stock: 'ghi'
}, {
  isEnabled: true,
  stock: 'jlk'
}]
```

We can do one better with combineLatest. If a function is passed in as the last parameter, combineLatest calls this projection function with a parameter for each latest value, and then passes whatever the function returns down the stream. It's like a built-in map operator. In our case, we'll filter out all the stocks the user disabled and pass on only an array of enabled symbols.

vanilla/advancedAsync/stocks-complete.ts
```
let settings$ = combineLatest(
  makeCheckboxStream(abcEl, 'ABC'),
  makeCheckboxStream(defEl, 'DEF'),
  makeCheckboxStream(ghiEl, 'GHI'),
  makeCheckboxStream(jklEl, 'JKL'),
  (...stockBoxes) => {
    return stockBoxes
      .filter(stockBox => stockBox.isEnabled)
      .map(stockBox => stockBox.stock);
  }
);
```

At this point, you have two separate streams—one containing all the information about the stock prices, and the other representing the latest data about which stocks the user actually cares about. We need the latest values from both streams. All that's needed is another combineLatest constructor and a projection function to keep the labels connected to the values in the stream:

vanilla/advancedAsync/stocks-complete.ts
```
combineLatest(
  settings$,
  stockStream$,
  (enabledStocks, stockUpdates) => ({ enabledStocks, stockUpdates })
)
```

While we could do the stock filtering in the projection function, I prefer to keep filtering and projection separate. Each operator should perform one action—this keeps confusion low and refactoring easy. The next snippet shows the `map` operator that takes the latest from the two streams and returns a list of updates that contains only the stocks the user has enabled:

vanilla/advancedAsync/stocks-complete.ts
```
.pipe(
  map(({ enabledStocks, stockUpdates }) => {
    return stockUpdates
      .filter(stockHistory => enabledStocks.includes(stockHistory.label));
  })
)
```

This new stream emits a new value every time there's new data about the stocks or visualization. Since this stream operates on a single event within the stream, it doesn't need to complicate things with an inner observable.

Finally, we can reuse the subscribe method from before—the final result of these streams is the same: a collection of data points on stock price.

vanilla/advancedAsync/stocks-complete.ts
```
.subscribe(newDataSet => {
  config.data.datasets = newDataSet;
  stockChart.update();
}, err => console.error(err));
```

What We've Learned

If you've learned anything from this chapter, it's that Rx has an operator for pretty much everything. By now you should be comfortable with writing observables and using them to solve both synchronous and asynchronous problems. I wouldn't worry about remembering Every Single Operator—you can always look those up in the docs.

So far you've only dealt with observables where a second subscribe triggers a whole new observable stream. In the next chapter, you'll learn how to split observables while maintaining only one origin. See you there!

CHAPTER 5

Multiplexing Observables

So far you've learned that a new subscriber creates an entirely new observable stream, including rerunning the constructor. The term for this kind of observable is a *cold* observable, and it's the default in RxJS. However, sometimes you may want to create only a single source for an observable stream (such as the websocket example in *Advanced Async*). You don't want to create a pile of new websocket connections if all of a page's components want to listen in on the stream. In this case, you need a *hot* observable.

A hot observable contains a single stream that every subscriber listens in on (this is called *multicasting*). These hot observables can be created by piping through publish on a regular observable or by creating a subject, which are hot by default. This sounds complicated, but if you take it step-by-step, you'll do just fine. You'll learn these concepts by building this chapter's big project: a chat system. Time to dive in!

The Problem with Cold Observables

So far, you've learned that each new subscription to an observable runs the root creation function:

```
let myObs$ = new Observable(o => {
  console.log('Creation Function');
  setInterval(() => o.next('hello', Math.random()), 1000);
});

myObs$.subscribe(x => console.log('streamA', x));

setTimeout(() => {
  myObs$.subscribe(x => console.log('streamB', x));
}, 500);
```

When you run the above snippet, you see Creation Function logged to the console twice, showing that you've created two entirely separate observable streams.

Each observable stream sees hello at different times, with separate random numbers attached. Rx does this by default to ensure every stream is isolated from every other stream, keeping your code manageable.

On the other hand, sometimes you don't want to trigger the creation logic every time another part of your application wants to listen in on the result. Consider an AJAX request that fetches a user object:

```
let user$ = ajax('/user');
```

You might naively pass around user$ to all the components in your application, where all of the listeners happily subscribe and pull whatever information they need. This solution works until the backend engineer comes chasing after us with a pile of excessive log files demanding to know why every page load makes seventeen requests to the /user endpoint. Oops. That's because observables are "cold" by default—each new subscription creates an entire new observable and stream of data. In this case, each subscribe makes an independent request to the backend for the same data.

Cold Observable (default)

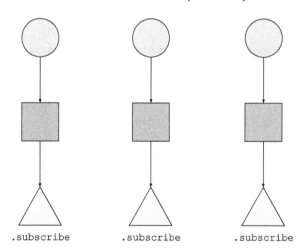

.subscribe   .subscribe   .subscribe

You need something to *multiplex* your data—to make a single request but distribute it to multiple subscribers as shown in the figure on page 61.

Fortunately, RxJS provides a multitude of options. The simplest one is the share operator, which is called on a single, cold observable stream and converts the stream into a hot stream. This conversion doesn't happen immediately; share waits until there's at least one subscriber and then subscribes to the original observable (triggering the AJAX request). Further subscriptions do

Hot Observable (Subject)

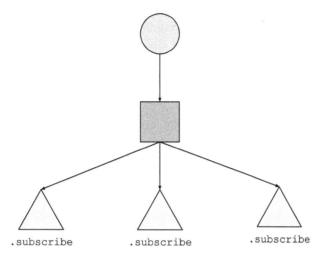

not create a new observable; instead they all listen in to the data that the original subscription produces. Updating the "Creation Function" example, you'll see:

```
vanilla/multiplexingObservables/share.ts
import { Observable } from 'rxjs';
import { share } from 'rxjs/operators';

let myObs$ = new Observable(o => {
  console.log('Creation Function');
  setInterval(() => o.next('hello ' + Math.random()), 1000);
})
  .pipe(
    share()
  );

myObs$.subscribe(x => console.log('streamA', x));

setTimeout(() => {
  myObs$.subscribe(x => console.log('streamB', x));
}, 500);
```

share is a good tool to use when new listeners don't care about previous data (like in the stock market example). Unfortunately for our RxJS loving users, the following still doesn't work:

```
let user$ = ajax('/user')
.pipe(share());
```

The first component that subscribes to user$ triggers a request to the server. When the request finishes, all subscribers are given the returned data simultaneously. Anyone who subscribes after the initial request finishes is plumb out of luck. One solution is to delay the triggering of the request. When a stream is multiplexed with share, the trigger is the first subscriber. An alternative solution is to manually trigger the subscription by breaking the multiplexing into two parts: publish and connect.

publish converts our unicasted observable into a multicasted one but adds no additional logic around subscribing like share does. Instead, the publish operator won't do anything until there's a manual trigger to start the stream. The manual trigger is a call to the connect method.

```
// A multicasted observable you can pass to all of our components
let users$ = ajax('/user')
.pipe(publish());

// Once all of our components are subscribed
user$.connect();
```

Using publish and connect allows for fine-grained control over when an observable finally starts. This control can be enormously powerful when tuning for performance or in cases like lazy loading where you can avoid triggering requests until the user loads a particular section of your application.

Behind the scenes, both share and publish/connect use the Subject class. Understanding subjects is the final step to unlocking all that RxJS has to offer you.

Multicasting with the Subject Class

At its core, a Subject acts much like a regular observable, but each subscription is hooked into the same source, like the publish/share example. Subjects also are observers and have next, error, and done methods to send data to all subscribers at once:

```
let mySubject = new Subject();

mySubject.subscribe(val => console.log('Subscription 1:', val));
mySubject.subscribe(val => console.log('Subscription 2:', val));

mySubject.next(42);

/*
  Console output:
  Subscription 1: 42
  Subscription 2: 42
*/
```

Because subjects are observers, they can be passed directly into a subscribe call, and all the events from the original observable will be sent through the subject to its subscribers.

```
let mySubject = new Subject();

mySubject.subscribe(val => console.log(val));

let myObservable = interval(1000);

// Multicast myObservable's data through mySubject
myObservable.subscribe(mySubject);
```

Any Subject can *subscribe* to a regular observable and multicast the values flowing through it.

The general-purpose solution to our AJAX problem is an AsyncSubject, a specialized Subject that keeps track of the source observable and waits for it to complete. Then, and only then, does it pass on the resulting value to all subscribers. It also stores the value, and hands it to any new subscribers who jump in after the initial request is complete. Finally, we have a generalized solution for the user data AJAX problem:

```
let user$ = ajax('/user');
let asyncSub = new AsyncSubject();
user$.subscribe(asyncSub);

asyncSub.subscribe(val => console.log('sub 1:', val.response));

// If the request completes before the subscription,
//    the subscription will still be called with the result
setTimeout(() => {
  asyncSub.subscribe(val => console.log('sub 2:', val.response));
}, 3000);
```

The first line creates an AJAX observable that points to the /user endpoint. The second line creates as a new instance of the AsyncSubject class. Since any Subject has next, error, and done methods, we can pass asyncSub directly into the subscribe call off of user$ on the third line. This subscribe immediately triggers the request to the backend. Before the call completes, a subscription to asyncSub is created. Nothing is logged until the request completes.

Once the server responds with the data, user$ passes it on to the single subscriber: asyncSub. At this point, two things happen. asyncSub emits to all current subscribers an event containing the response data, and it also records that data for itself. Later, when the setTimeout executes, asyncSub emits the same data to the second subscription.

Building a Chat Room

Chat systems are a favorite practice realm for programmers. You need to build out a two-way communications backbone, as well as a reactive UI on top of it. Subjects can help you enormously, handling both the real-time communication and data storage for use by components initialized after load. An example of this would be a subject recording the chat history in the background so that when the user opens that room, they'll see the most recent messages without needing an additional request.

This excercise is a capstone project for everything you've learned so far in this book. The goal is to connect many reactive streams to build an entire application. Extraneous functions to perform the raw DOM manipulation around displaying messages and modals are provided for you in chatlib.ts. While you're encouraged to take a look at these functions, they will not be discussed further, so we can keep the focus on learning RxJS.

When you're finished with this section, the chat application will have a login system, multiple rooms, and a chat history for each room.

This chat system is centered around a single subject hooked up to the chat websocket. You'll use the webSocket constructor for connecting and managing this connection to the server. Add the following snippet to the reader.ts file in the chapter directory. The chatStream$ variable will serve as the central source of information for your chat system.

```
vanilla/multiplexingObservables/reader-complete.ts
interface ChatRoom {
  name: string;
}
interface ChatMessage {
  room: ChatRoom;
}
let wsUrl = 'ws://localhost:3000/api/multiplexingObservables/chat-ws';
let chatStream$ = webSocket<ChatMessage>(wsUrl);
```

This chat application has four parts, and each one hooks into chatStream$ in a unique way. The first section handles the user providing a username as a rudimentary form of authentication.

Logging in

The first thing you will see when you load the page is a modal that asks for a username. In this section, you add code that allows the user to enter a username, connect to the server to log in, and close the modal to display the rest of the page. Let's add some code that listens in on the events from that modal to trigger login. To make it easy on the user, you'll create two different observables, one listening for the Enter key, and the other listening for a click on the Login button. All the code cares about at this point is that the user has filled in their name and wishes to submit it.

At this point, we map to the value of the input box (ignoring any value, the important thing is that an event happened), filter out empty strings, and display a handy loading spinner to indicate to the user that the backend is working hard on getting their chat ready. Finally, the subscription calls authenticateUser—a function you'll create in the next snippet.

```
vanilla/multiplexingObservables/reader-complete.ts
interface User {
  rooms: ChatRoom[];
}
let userSubject$ = new AsyncSubject<User>();
function authenticateUser(username) {
  let user$ = ajax(
        'http://localhost:3000/api/multiplexingObservables/chat/user/'
        + username)
    .pipe(
      map(data => data.response)
    );

  user$.subscribe(userSubject$);
}
```

Next, let's use an AJAX observable to tell the backend about the newly connected user. The AjaxObservable sends a request to the backend, and the AsyncSubject listens in, storing the resulting value for the rest of the application to use upon request.

vanilla/multiplexingObservables/reader-complete.ts

```
merge(
  fromEvent(loginBtn, 'click'),
  fromEvent<any>(loginInput, 'keypress')
  .pipe(
    // Ignore all keys except for enter
    filter(e => e.keyCode === 13)
  )
)
.pipe(
  map(() => loginInput.value),
  filter(Boolean),
  tap(showLoadingSpinner)
)
.subscribe(authenticateUser);
```

Joe asks:
What's with the Boolean Filter?

To review: The filter method expects to take a function that checks the latest value in the stream and returns true or false. filter only passes on a value if the function returns true.

JavaScript provides constructor functions for all of the primitives in the language, including booleans. The Boolean constructor takes any value, returning true if the value is truthy, and false otherwise. Sound familiar? .filter(Boolean) can be used as a shortcut for .filter(value => !!value) and carries a clearer intent for what you intend to do.

Now the code knows when the user has chosen a username and now it needs to close the modal and show the rest of the app. To do so, add a subscription to the user subject, calling the provided closeLoginModal function when the user request finishes and providing data about the current state of the chat room.

vanilla/multiplexingObservables/reader-complete.ts

```
userSubject$
.subscribe(closeLoginModal);
```

Now, you should be able to load the page, enter a username in the modal, and wait for the backend to respond with data about the current state of the chat. After the backend responds, nothing is listening in to render anything to the page. It's time to implement the code around viewing and switching chat rooms.

Rendering and Switching Rooms

After the user has logged in, they will want to see all of the rooms available to them and switch between them. To accomplish this, once the login modal has closed, start listening in for any new messages that come across the websocket. While it's possible to not keep any history and only show the latest messages, you can use the RxJS ReplaySubject to track room history. A Replay-Subject records the last n events and plays them back to every new subscriber. In this example, we'll create a new ReplaySubject for every chat channel and create a new subscription whenever the user switches rooms.

```
vanilla/multiplexingObservables/reader-complete.ts
function makeRoomStream(roomName) {
  let roomStream$ = new ReplaySubject(100);
  chatStream$
  .pipe(
    filter(msg => msg.room.name === roomName)
  )
  .subscribe(roomStream$);
  return roomStream$;
}
```

When the user authenticates, the server replies with the list of rooms the user is currently in. The room section needs to listen in on that, render the list of room buttons to the page, create room streams using the function above, and trigger an event loading the user into the first room on the list by default. Here, you'll use three separate subscribe functions to keep things compartmentalized:

```
vanilla/multiplexingObservables/reader-complete.ts
let roomStreams = {};
userSubject$
.subscribe(userObj => {
  userObj.rooms.forEach(room =>
    roomStreams[room.name] = makeRoomStream(room.name)
  );
});
userSubject$
  .subscribe(userObj => renderRoomButtons(userObj.rooms));
userSubject$
  .subscribe(userObj => roomLoads$.next(userObj.rooms[0].name));
```

For that code to work, you need to track when the user clicks one of the room buttons on the left, indicating they'd like to switch to a new room. A separate subject is created to track room loads so that we can trigger a room load from an event emitted by userSubject$. There's also a check to see whether the user clicked directly on the unread number, in which case, we pass on the parent element.

```
vanilla/multiplexingObservables/reader-complete.ts
let roomClicks$ = fromEvent<any>(roomList, 'click')
.pipe(
  // If they click on the number, pass on the button
  map(event => {
    if (event.target.tagName === 'SPAN') {
      return event.target.parentNode;
    }
    return event.target;
  }),
  // Remove unread number from room name text
  map(element => element.innerText.replace(/\s\d+$/, ''))
);

let roomLoads$ = new Subject();
roomClicks$.subscribe(roomLoads$);
```

Finally, now that you're tracking which room is active, it's time to start listening in on the streams and showing new messages on the page. The roomLoads$ stream listens for new room loads, updates the DOM classes on the buttons, switches to the new room stream through switchMap, and writes each event from the stream to the page as a message (writeMessageToPage and setActiveRoom are provided for you in chatLib.ts). Remember that each stream in roomStreams is a ReplaySubject, so as soon as switchMap subscribes to the subject, the last 100 messages are passed down the chain.

```
vanilla/multiplexingObservables/reader-complete.ts
roomLoads$
.pipe(
  tap(setActiveRoom),
  switchMap(room => roomStreams[room])
)
.subscribe(writeMessageToPage);
```

Now that you've completed this section of the application, a list of rooms to join appears on the left, and each room starts to display messages from other users. When a user clicks the button to switch to a new room, the chat history that's been collected so far is shown. While this is starting to look like a functional chat room, one critical feature is missing: the user still can't send a message to a chat room. Time to fix that.

Sending Messages

Now that the user can see the current rooms and the messages sent to them, it's time to let them send messages of their own. Compared to the two sections in the chat room so far, sending messages is fairly simple. It starts with the same technique as the login modal, using merge to listen for either a selection of the Send button or a press of the Enter key. Next, the stream plucks out the value of the message box, ensures the value is not an empty string, and resets the message box.

The following snippet introduces a new operator you haven't seen before: withLatestFrom. The stream in this snippet needs to send a new chat message (entered by the user) to the server and needs to annotate it with the user's name and current room so the server knows who sent the message and where it was sent.

Previously, you used combineLatest whenever you needed to combine the most recent value from multiple streams. combineLatest comes with a catch, though—it emits a new value when any of the streams emits a value. We don't want to send a new chat message when the user switches to a new room. Instead, withLatestFrom only emits new values when the observable stream that it's passed into through pipe emits a value. You can also add an optional projection function to combine the latest values from all of the streams.

```
vanilla/multiplexingObservables/reader-complete.ts
merge(
  fromEvent<any>(sendBtn, 'click'),
  fromEvent<any>(msgBox, 'keypress')
  .pipe(
    // Only emit event when enter key is pressed
    filter(e => e.keyCode === 13)
  )
)
.pipe(
  map(() => msgBox.value),
  filter(Boolean),
  tap(() => msgBox.value = ''),
  withLatestFrom(
    roomLoads$,
    userSubject$,
    (message, room, user) => ({ message, room, user })
  )
)
.subscribe(val => chatStream$.next(<any>val));
```

Finally, the chat room is feature complete. Users can log in, read incoming messages in all rooms in the system, and send messages of their own. Time to add a final flourish: let's display how many unread messages are waiting in each room.

Displaying Unread Notifications

While not strictly needed for a chat room, it can be interesting to see how many new messages have shown up in a room that the user doesn't have directly loaded. This feature is concerned with two streams: new messages and room loads. The tricky part is that, while we want to listen in to multiple streams and store state inside the observable stream (using merge and scan), we also want to perform different actions depending on which stream emits a new value. To make this simple, call map on the streams as they're passed into the merge constructor, so each new event tells us what type of event it is:

vanilla/multiplexingObservables/reader-complete.ts
```
merge(
  chatStream$.pipe(
    map(msg => ({type: 'message', room: msg.room.name}))
  ),
  roomLoads$.pipe(
    map(room => ({type: 'roomLoad', room: room}))
  )
)
```

Now that the stream is annotated, you can use scan to carry the state of all unread messages. Here the state contains two properties: rooms, an object storing the number of unread messages per room, and activeRoom, the most recently loaded room. Inside scan, we check to see what type of event has been emitted.

In case the event is a room load, the state is updated to record the new active room and set the number of unread messages in that room to 0. In the case that the websocket has sent a new message, scan first checks to see whether the message was sent to the current room. If it was, the current state is returned unmodified. Otherwise, we make sure that the current state has a record for the room in question (adding a new entry if this is the first time scan has seen this room, to allow for a dynamic room list). Finally, the room record is incremented.

vanilla/multiplexingObservables/reader-complete.ts
```
.pipe(
  scan((unread, event: any) => {
    // new message in room
    if (event.type === 'roomLoad') {
      unread.activeRoom = event.room;
      unread.rooms[event.room] = 0;
    } else if (event.type === 'message') {
      if (event.room === unread.activeRoom) {
        return unread;
      }
      if (!unread.rooms[event.room]) {
        unread.rooms[event.room] = 0;
      }
      unread.rooms[event.room]++;
    }
```

```
  return unread;
}, {
  rooms: {},
  activeRoom: ''
}),
```

The last step has two `map` operators to convert the state from `scan` into something easier to loop over, and the subscribe call passes each room object to `setUnread`, a function from `chatlib.ts` that updates the text in the room buttons.

```
vanilla/multiplexingObservables/reader-complete.ts
  map(unread => unread.rooms),
  map(rooms =>
    Object.keys(rooms)
    .map(key => ({
      roomName: key,
      number: rooms[key]
    }))
  )
)
.subscribe(roomArr => {
  roomArr.forEach(setUnread);
});
```

With that, your chat room is complete. If you're looking for a bit more of a challenge, try to update the code so that the user can change their name. Right now, this codebase assumes that the user can't change their username after entering it in the initial modal. Imagine if `userSubject$` was an unbounded stream, adding an AJAX call for each username change. How would you change things to make them more flexible? Start with the pattern you used to track unread rooms, since that brought in two unbounded streams.

What We Learned

This was the biggest application you've built so far. Congratulations for making it all the way through. At this point, you should understand how observables can be single or multicasted and under what situations one would use either option. You also got some hands-on experience with Subjects in general, and Async/Replay subjects specifically.

A larger issue with the codebase you've accumulated is that it's very dependent on global variables, with very little organization. In the next few chapters, you'll start using Angular as a framework to properly structure your code. Angular also relies on Rx to handle all of an application's events, allowing you to do even more with observables, such as validating forms and dealing with shaky network connections.

CHAPTER 6

Using HTTP in Angular

While the chat example in *Multiplexing Observables* was a good chance to stretch your Rx muscles, the lack of a coherent framing to structure the application was already showing. A list of functions sufficed for a barebones chat, but this would quickly become unwieldy as more pages and functionality were added. In fact, no serious web application should be built purely with observables. Observables work best as a glue connecting your application together, and no one wants to live in a house made entirely of glue.

In the next few chapters, you'll learn how to work with Angular, a modern framework that has RxJS integrated into its core. While these chapters focus on using Angular, the techniques covered are useful regardless of the supporting framework you choose.

The project for this chapter covers scaffolding an Angular app, using the Rx-based HttpClient to communicate with a backend, routing through a single page app, and listening in to routing events to collect analytics data. You'll build out a Pinterest-like application. The user will search through images, collect the ones they like, and tag them for easier searching later. For an example of what it'll look like when you're finished, see the screenshot on page 74.

Using the Code Provided for this Section

All of the code for this section resides in the ng2 folder of the code you downloaded from The Pragmatic Bookshelf site. For most projects in this section, you'll build things from scratch (the exception is the performance demo in *Advanced Angular*). The complete apps are in the folder if you get stuck. Don't forget to run npm install in each project, if you want to run it live.

This is the first chapter about Angular, so you'll be introduced to a few concepts from that world. While this book covers many Angular concepts, it's not a comprehensive introduction. Some Angular experience is helpful, but not required to understand this section. First, let's learn about generating new projects with the Angular CLI.

Joe asks:

Wait, Which Angular Are We Talking about Here?

Confusingly, two different frameworks are named Angular. In short, Angular 1 (now known as AngularJS) was first released in October of 2010. There have been many releases since then. Google then took the lessons of AngularJS and wrote a new framework, named Angular (note the lack of "JS" at the end), starting with major version 2. Colloquially, this became known as Angular 2. However, Google's engineers wanted to maintain Semantic Versioning with this new framework, which requires that the major version be incremented for each breaking change. In the case of this section of the book, we'll use Angular, specifically version 6.0.3.

Alas, this is confusing, but as AngularJS' popularity wanes, things will become clearer, and we can all take advantage of the security in knowing that non-major releases won't break our apps.

Generating a New Project

Angular supports many powerful tools like server-side compilation and service workers. Using these advanced tools requires a specific project structure and build chain. Keeping track of all these details while simultaneously developing new features can be a thankless task. Fortunately, the Angular team has bundled up all their best practices into a command-line generator that allows us to easily create new components while still adhering to best practices. Install it globally with: npm install -g @angular/cli. (This book uses version 6.0.8 of the Angular CLI.) You'll use it throughout the Angular section of this book.

Using the Angular CLI

With that in mind, let's use the CLI to bootstrap this chapter's project: a photo gallery. This project will provide lots of opportunities to connect dynamic loading with the interactivity of the page. The user can view their photo gallery as well as specific photos, and edit details about each photo. To start off the app, run ng new rx-photos --routing in the directory you want to create the app in. The new command generates a brand-new Angular application, along with all of the scaffolding needed to build and serve that application. The --routing parameter tells ng to also add in observable-powered routing for this single-page app.

Move into your newly created directory and browse around a bit. The CLI generated a basic app, along with tests and other infrastructure. Take a look at package.json to see what tasks can be run with your new app. When you're satisfied with your directory browsing, return to the root of the project and run ng serve to fire up a server for the photo project. Browse to http://locahost:4200, and you see a demo page showing that you've set everything up correctly as seen in the screenshot on page 76.

Once the server is up and running, it's time to generate the rest of the scaffolding for your photo application. The eventual goal of this application is to allow a user to search, browse, save, and tag photos. This requires three pages:

- Searching and browsing photo results
- Viewing saved photos
- Editing and tagging photos

Welcome to app!

Here are some links to help you start:

- Tour of Heroes
- CLI Documentation
- Angular blog

\\// Joe asks:
≿ **What If I Don't See the Demo Page?**

You might not see the demo page for several reasons. Here are some debugging tips to get you started:

- Wait a bit. Especially on older computers, the initial compile step might take some time.

- Make sure you're using the latest version of the ngcli by reinstalling ngcli and rerunning the serve command.

- To remove and reinstall your dependencies, run rm -r node_modules && npm i at the project root.

Each page requires a root component to control that page. The ng tool can create a new item from a base schematic and add it to your application with the generate command. In this case, the goal is to generate components, so the command works like this:

```
ng generate component search-header
CREATE src/app/search-header/search-header.component.css (0 bytes)
CREATE src/app/search-header/search-header.component.html (32 bytes)
CREATE src/app/search-header/search-header.component.spec.ts (671 bytes)
CREATE src/app/search-header/search-header.component.ts (296 bytes)
```

You don't need to type out the full command every time. The command above could be shortened to ng g c search-header.

The photo project needs more than one component. Generate components named results-list,saved-list and edit-photo. One final thing: copy the contents of index.html—from the finished project included with this book—into the same file in your project. The contents include some styles to make your app look a bit better, so you can focus on the observable side of things. Assets are loaded from the project server, so make sure you have that running.

You've now created the five components that the photo application will use. The browser still displays the same old page; to get these new components to display, we need to modify the HTML found in app.component.html. Fortunately, adding a new component is easy. Delete all of the generated HTML and enter the following:

ng2/rx-photos/src/app/app.component.html
```
<app-search-header>
</app-search-header>
```

Now that app-search-header is being rendered to the page, let's put some content in it. Add this to search-header.component.html:

ng2/rx-photos/src/app/search-header/search-header.component.html
```
<header>
  <div class="search-container">
    <input class="search" placeholder="Search..."
        autofocus [formControl]="searchQuery">
  </div>
</header>
```

At this point, the page has a green header bar with a search box. The search box won't work; time to hook that up by importing the tools needed, starting with HttpClient.

Angular provides its own client for working with AJAX requests. In fact, it provides *two* such clients. The original one, Http, is deprecated. It had a solid core, but interacting with it was clunky and repetitive. The new tool, HttpClient brings several advantages.

First, it assumes that a response will be JSON, saving tedious time writing out .map(response => response.json()) for every request. It also accepts a generic type, further improving our editor's awareness of what's going on. Finally, it resurrects HttpInterceptors from AngularJS (unfamiliar with HttpInterceptors? You'll find out later in this chapter). There's a lot packed up in this little library, so let's get started.

Since HttpClient is new to the Angular ecosystem, it's not included by default. We need to explicitly import the module in the root app module (Angular modules represent a collection of components, services and other modules). Open app.module.ts and add the following lines:

```
import { BrowserModule } from '@angular/platform-browser';
import { NgModule } from '@angular/core';
import { AppComponent } from './app.component';
import { PhoneNumComponent } from './phone-num/phone-num.component';
import { HttpClientModule } from '@angular/common/http';
import {FormsModule, ReactiveFormsModule} from '@angular/forms';

@NgModule({
  declarations: [
    AppComponent,
    PhoneNumComponent
  ],
  imports: [
    BrowserModule,
    HttpClientModule
    FormsModule,
    ReactiveFormsModule
  ],
  providers: [],
  bootstrap: [AppComponent]
})
export class AppModule { }
```

❶ First, import the http module into the file. This is included with the @angular/common package, so there's no need to install more packages.

❷ At this point, add the import for reactive forms as well, which will be used later in this chapter.

❸ Once the modules are imported into the file, they need to be passed into the module declaration, so all of the components and services in this module can access the variables the previously imported modules export.

Now that app.module.ts has been updated, we can import HttpClient into a service. Generate a service inside your project with ng g service photos. This service contains most of the work we do in this chapter. In Angular, services are where the heavy data lifting happens. Components should be used to translate data to and from the view.

Open the newly-created photos.service.ts file. The Angular CLI has generated the outline of a service:

```
import { Injectable } from '@angular/core';

@Injectable({
  providedIn: 'root'
})
export class PhotosService {

  constructor() { }
}
```

Joe asks:
What Does providedIn Mean?

An Angular app can be made up of any number of modules. These modules can be split up and dynamically loaded on the frontend as needed. Angular needs to know which module we want our service to be under. Providing a service in root means that the entire application can access a single, shared instance of this service (and is the default option).

The first order of business is to bring in HttpClient. There are two steps for injecting anything in Angular. The first is to import the class from the Angular library itself. This import is used for type hinting as well as informing Angular what needs to be injected:

```
import { HttpClient } from '@angular/common/http';
```

Editor autoimports

Some editors automatically import variables as you type them in your file. When this happens, be sure you're not importing HttpClient from selenium-webdriver/http, which is also installed as part of the default Angular setup.

The second is to add a private parameter to the constructor function, named whatever we like, with the type of the class we just injected:

ng2/rx-photos/src/app/photos.service.ts
```
api = 'http://localhost:3000/api/ng2ajax';
constructor(private http: HttpClient) { }
```

To make things easier, an api property is also added above the constructor, detailing the URL of the API that these HTTP requests will hit. If the URL of the API ever changes, only one update needs to be made.

The type annotation on http is required, so the Angular compiler knows what to inject into the service when it is initially created. The private label is added so TypeScript knows that it should be attached to the this of our object. Now that we have access to the client, it's time to use it. The simplest use of HttpClient is a GET request:

```
http.get(someURL)
.subscribe({
  next: result => console.log(result),
  err: err => console.err(err),
  done: () => console.log('request finished')
});
```

This looks remarkably similar to the earlier work with the ajax constructor. However, there's a structural change, now that you're working in Angular—*the service should not subscribe*. Remember, observables are lazy. The service doesn't want to make any requests until it's sure there's a component that wants to know about the results. Instead of doing everything in a single method, we'll add a method that does everything *up to* the subscribe and returns the observable. Later on, any component that wants to request data will add the subscription.

```
searchPhotos(searchQuery: string): Observable<IPhoto[]> {
    return this.http.get(this.api + '/imgSearch/' + searchQuery);
}
```

Return Annotations

The new syntax after the closing parenthesis in the function argument is a type annotation declaring what that function returns. In this case, searchPhotos returns an Observable. The function doesn't return just any observable, the declaration can also specify the type of the events that observable emits. In this case, each event from the observable contains an array of IPhotos. Type-Script doesn't know what an IPhoto is, so you'll see an error in the console when Angular tries to compile this file. Let's use TypeScript's interface keyword to define what an IPhoto is. Add this to the top of your file, below the import declarations.

```
export interface IPhoto {
  url: string;
  id: any;
}
```

This interface declares that anything with the type IPhoto will have a url property set to a string and an id property, which can be anything. This also implicitly declares that anything IPhoto will not have any additional properties. This interface is exported so that other components can use it. TypeScript also allows you to define optional properties by adding a question mark to the name of the property. If we'd wanted a third, optional property called name, we could have added it like so: name?: string;.

While syntactically correct, this method will still raise complaints from Type-Script. The annotation claims that the method returns an Observable, which it does, but specfically, an observable where every event contains an array of objects conforming to the IPhoto interface. By default, HttpClient returns a much blander type: Observable<Object>—not what we want. With the old Http service, a lot of type casting would be needed to achieve this. The new HttpClient accepts a generic type where the developer can specify exactly what's coming back in the AJAX request at the point where it's made:

```
searchPhotos(searchQuery: string) {
  return this.http.get<IPhoto[]>(this.api + '/imgSearch/' + searchQuery);
}
```

TypeScript is smart enough that it figures out what's coming back from the defintion on this.http.get<IPhoto[]>, which means that the method doesn't need to explicity define a returned type. Now that a method is making an AJAX call, let's build out the components to put that data on the page.

Displaying Returned Data

Open search-header.component.ts, which was generated for you earlier, along with its template search-header.component.html. In the template, you can see that the input element has a [formControl] attribute. You'll learn more about FormControl and the related services in *Building Reactive Forms in Angular*. For now, all we need to know is that it's an observable that emits the current value of the search bar whenever the value of the input element changes. Your first task is to connect the input element to the component. Import the FormControl class from @angular/forms and add the following property declaration to your header component.

```
import { FormControl } from '@angular/forms';
import { PhotosService } from '../photos.service';

export class SearchHeaderComponent implements OnInit {
  searchQuery = new FormControl();
  constructor(private photos: PhotosService) { }
```

❶ This declares the searchQuery property on the class and sets the value to a new instance of FormControl.

❷ Finally, the component needs to know how to fetch the photos. Import the PhotosService and inject it into the component in the constructor method so the component can request new photos on every search change.

Now that the component can subscribe to changes in the search bar, it's time to trigger a new search every time the input changes, much like the typeahead example from *Advanced Async*. Add the following to the ngOnInit method:

```
ngOnInit() {
  this.searchQuery.valueChanges
  .pipe(
    debounceTime(333),
    switchMap(query =>
      this.photos.searchPhotos(query)
    )
  )
  .subscribe(photoList =>
    console.log('New search results:', photoList)
  );
}
```

❶ This observable emits each time the user changes the value in the search bar.

❷ To avoid making too many AJAX requests in a short time, debounceTime is added, waiting 1/3 of a second before doing anything. If another event is emitted in that time, the timer is reset.

❸ When the user pauses typing, tell the photo-fetching service to initiate another API request.

The page will auto-refresh with your changes. Type some gibberish in the search box; if you can see the logs in the console, the search is triggering correctly. Two parts down, one to go.

The final piece of the puzzle is results-list.component.ts. Open that file and import the photo search service like before (don't forget to add it to the constructor as well). The component now has access to photo search service, but all the photo search service can do is search. The subscription lies in the header component—there's no way to access it in the results list. Instead, the photo search service needs to be upgraded using a subject to allow it to share new results with any component that wants to subscribe. In this case, the photo search service uses a BehaviorSubject.

A BehaviorSubject is a simplified version of the ReplaySubject you used back in *Multiplexing Observables*. Whereas the ReplaySubject stored an arbitrary number of events, the BehaviorSubject only records the value of the latest event. Whenever a BehaviorSubject records a new subscription, it emits the latest value to the subscriber as well as any new values that are passed in. The BehaviorSubject is useful when dealing with single units of state, such as configuration options, or in this example, the latest photos returned from the API. The application never needs to know previous states, just the latest photos to show.

Go back to photos.service.ts and make the following modifications (you'll also need to import BehaviorSubject, by importing either all of RxJS or just BehaviorSubject specifically):

```
@Injectable({
  providedIn: 'root'
})
export class PhotosService {
  latestPhotos = new BehaviorSubject([]);
  constructor(private http: HttpClient) { }

  searchPhotos(searchQuery: string) {
    return this.http.get<IPhoto[]>('http://localhost:4567/photos/search?q='
      + searchQuery)
    .subscribe(photos => this.latestPhotos.next(photos));
  }
}
```

BehaviorSubject (like any subject) is an *observer* as well as an *observable*; it has a next method you can use to alert all listeners that there's new data. While searchPhotos could technically pass this.latestPhotos directly into the subscribe call, doing that would mean that latestPhotos will pick up on the completion of the AJAX call and call the done method. Since latestPhotos needs to be active through the entire life cycle of the program, the code ensures that only the next method is called.

Why are there just pictures of cats?

 It's no fun embarking on a programming project and then realizing the internet has gone out. The local server is smart enough to detect when problems happen and responds with pictures of cats, so you can keep on learning.

This is a simple web app, so sharing a subject in a service suffices for now (there's a race condition—can you find it?). In *Advanced Angular*, you'll learn about ngrx, a tool that will help you create apps with more scalable state management.

Now that the photos service is sharing the results of each search, you need to display those results on the page with the results-list component you generated earlier. First, go to app.module.html and add the results-list component to the page under app-search-header:

```
<results-list></results-list>
```

Next, update results-list.component.ts with the following changes, importing where needed:

```
export class ResultsListComponent implements OnInit {
  photos: IPhoto[];
  constructor(private photosService: PhotosService) { }

  ngOnInit() {
    this.photosService.latestPhotos
      .subscribe(photos => {
        this.photos = photos;
      });
  }
}
```

This acts like every other call to subscribe that you've seen in the book. However, there's a problem here—since the subject we're listening in on lives for the entire life cycle of the program, so will this subscription. Every time the user loads this view, another subscription will be added to latestPhotos, slowing down the application and resulting in some very grumpy users. One could monkey around by adding an ngOnDestroy method that unsubscribes, but there's a simpler way to do this: the async pipe.

Pipes in Angular

A massive chunk of frontend work can be summed up as, "Fetch data in format A, convert it to format B, display that to the user." Sometimes, we want to differentiate between a format that's easy for machines to manipulate (say, a Date object) and something that's easy for the user to understand (an easy-to-read "December 20th"). Angular pipes give us the power to separate the two without the headache that's involved in keeping two variables synced together.

These pipes are a tool used in the view, that take a value from the data model in the component, and transform it into what's actually shown on the page. The Date example would work something like this:

```
<div>Photo created on {{ photo.created | date }}</div>
```

The vertical bar is what gives pipes their name; it originally came from Unix terminal emulators. Angular comes with a set of predefined pipes, such as the DatePipe used above (other examples are the CurrencyPipe and JsonPipe). You can also define your own pipes through the CLI with ng g pipe pipe-name. For now, the focus is on the async pipe, which works with observables.

Remove all of the contents of ngOnInit in the result list component, as well as the declaration of the photos property. The async pipe will handle all of the manual subscription management. Open the view and add the pipe to the *ngFor loop:

```
<div *ngFor="let photo of photosService.latestPhotos | async">
```

The async pipe lets you treat observables as synchronous data—imagine it as a superpowered subscribe call that can only be used in the view. It also knows when it's no longer needed and cleans up any stray subscriptions so the app stays lean and fast, even after extended use. At this point, the basic search life cycle in your app should be working, but only to search photos. The next step is to use the HttpClient to send new data back to the server.

Saving New Data

Once the user has decided which photos they'd like to save, they need a functioning Save button. Time to hook the Save button up to PhotosService so that the backend can store photos the user would like to recall and edit later.

Clearing saved photos

 If you want to clear the saved photo database at any point, it's stored in photos.json in the asset-server directory.

Time to add a new method to the PhotosService that sends information about a new photo to the server, which will add the photo to the database. HttpClient provides a post method to send a POST request. The first parameter (like get) is the URL to send the request to, and the second is the request body:

```
ng2/rx-photos/src/app/photos.service.ts
addNewPhoto(photoUrl: string) {
  this.http.post<IPhoto>(this.api + '/addNewPhoto', {
    url: photoUrl
  })
    .subscribe();
}
```

In this case, the function has an empty subscribe call so that the request will be made. In a production application, a centralized error handler could be passed in to every otherwise-empty call to subscribe. Now that there's a method for saving a photo, it's time to connect it to the results list view. Parentheses around an event name is Angular's syntax for "Run this code when this event happens." In this case, we want to call addNewPhoto whenever the user clicks Save:

```
ng2/rx-photos/src/app/results-list/results-list.component.html
<button class="btn btn-default results-btn"
  (click)="photosService.addNewPhoto(photoUrl)">Save</button>
```

Now that the user can save photos, it's time to introduce routing between multiple components so the user can view and edit the photos they've saved.

Routing to Components

Angular, like most modern frameworks, uses the Single-Page App model. That is, instead of loading a new page every time the user navigates around a site, a scaffold is built on the initial page load, and then only what's necessary is swapped out on every navigation. This means the user can go from the photo search page to editing a photo's tags without reloading any of the root CSS, the page header, and other common services.

In your forays through the generated app.module.html, you may have noticed the <router-outlet> element. This element is used to tell Angular where the content of each page should be loaded (note that the page header is located outside the <router-outlet>). Angular comes with a built-in router powered by Rx to handle all of our page transitions.

In this section, we'll refactor the existing components to use routing and then build out routes for several new components. To start, we need to remove the results list component from app.component.html, which should now look like this:

ng2/rx-photos/src/app/app.component.html
```
<app-search-header>
</app-search-header>
<router-outlet></router-outlet>
```

Open app-routing.module.ts. This file was generated as part of the original app generation when we added the routing parameter to the ng new command. This routing file creates a separate module exclusively to handle all of your app's routing. The key section of the file is the routes array, currently empty:

```
const routes: Routes = [];
```

Right now it doesn't handle any routes at all. Time to change that. In the Angular routing model, each route is defined by a single root component. The first route that needs to be defined uses the ResultsListComponent that you wrote in the first half of this chapter. Add a route for the default path to render ResultsListComponent:

```
① import { ResultsListComponent } from './results-list.component';
② const routes: Routes = [{
     path: '',
     component: ResultsListComponent
   }];
```

❶ Unlike some of the routing options from AngularJS, the default Angular
router requires us to directly pass the component into the router config
step, so we need to import the actual class.

❷ This declares that when the root path is loaded, the router is to instantiate
the ResultsListComponent wherever the router-outlet element is found.

The app has returned to its original functionality without the need to hardcode
a location for our results list. Make sure to delete the
line in app.component.html so the homepage won't have two sets of results. Next,
add in routes for the other two components that were generated earlier.

```
ng2/rx-photos/src/app/app-routing.module.ts
import { ResultsListComponent } from './results-list/results-list.component';
import { SavedListComponent } from './saved-list/saved-list.component';
import { EditPhotoComponent } from './edit-photo/edit-photo.component';

const routes: Routes = [{
  path: '',
  component: ResultsListComponent
}, {
  path: 'savedphotos',
  component: SavedListComponent
}, {
  path: 'edit/:photoId',
  component: EditPhotoComponent
}];
```

In one of the new paths, there's a new syntax: a colon before the name of the
parameter. This means that a user browsing to /edit/12345 still ends up on a
page controlled by the EditPhotoComponent. The page knows that the photo to be
edited has the id 12345. The stream of changes to the route parameters are
provided to the component as an observable.

Linking Between Components

Now that the application has several components to handle, we need some way
of linking between them. To do this, we use the routerLink directive, which allows
us to use regular <a> tags like usual, but also hooks in all the niceties from the
router. Much like the href attribute, we pass the route we want to link to:

```
<a routerLink="edit/{{photo.id}}">Edit</a>
```

The routerLink directive is not limited to just anchor tags—it can be attached
to virtually any clickable element. Open search-header.component.html and add a

routing bar with two routerLink attributes, which allow the user to navigate between the pages of this app.

ng2/rx-photos/src/app/search-header/search-header.component.html
```
<div class="container">
  <div class="row center-text">
    <div class="btn-group">
      <button type="button" class="btn btn-default"
        routerLink="/">Search Photos</button>
      <button type="button" class="btn btn-default"
        routerLink="/savedphotos">My Saved Photos</button>
    </div>
  </div>
</div>
```

Now that there's a route to SavedListComponent, it's time to make that component do something.

Displaying a List of Saved Photos

This component can fetch all saved photos from the backend, display them as a list, and let the user select photos to edit individually. It has a lot in common with the ResultsListComponent, though there are a few differences once you get into the details. The two main differences are that the photo variable is now an object (instead of a string), and the button below the photo routes to the edit photo page.

The next chunk of the project will exercise the skills you learned from building the ResultsListComponent, so I recommend that you attempt to build this component out before you take a peek at the completed code below. The one hint you will need is that the endpoint to retrieve all saved photos is located at http://localhost:3000/api/ng2ajax/savedPhotos.

Ready to check your work?

The first thing is to add a method to PhotosService that fetches a list of all saved photos.

ng2/rx-photos/src/app/photos.service.ts
```
getSavedPhotos() {
  return this.http.get<IPhoto[]>(this.api + '/savedPhotos');
}
```

After that's added, you need to inject PhotosService into SavedListComponent and add an observable property representing that call.

```
ng2/rx-photos/src/app/saved-list/saved-list.component.ts
export class SavedListComponent implements OnInit {

  savedPhotos$: Observable<IPhoto[]>;
  constructor(private photosService: PhotosService) { }

  ngOnInit() {
    this.savedPhotos$ = this.photosService.getSavedPhotos();
  }
}
```

> **Joe asks:**
> ## Why Can't I Just Call getSavedPhotos Directly?
>
> It would reduce the boilerplate if we could just call getSavedPhotos directly in the view, but this doesn't work out the way we want. Whenever there's a change, Angular needs to double-check that the values in the view layer haven't changed. If getSavedPhotos is called in the view, Angular dutifully calls it whenever Angular checks for changes. This change detection cycle can be triggered by many things, one of which is an AJAX call completing. So if checking the view makes an AJAX call, and every time an AJAX completes, the view is checked, calling getSavedPhotos directly will result in an infinite loop and a very sad user. You'll read more about this change detection cycle (and the observables behind it) in *Advanced Angular*.

Finally, add the observable to the view (including the async pipe):

```
ng2/rx-photos/src/app/saved-list/saved-list.component.html
<div *ngFor="let photo of savedPhotos$ | async" class="result-container">
  <img [src]="photo.url" class="results-img" />
  <button class="btn btn-default results-btn"
    routerLink="/edit/{{ photo.id }}">Edit</button>
</div>
```

Now users can see an overview of all the photos they've saved so far. The last major task is to build out a page to edit individual photos.

Editing a Single Photo

Now that the user can search and save photos, it's time to add the final major component: editing a saved photo. The first requirement is simple—get a single photo from the API. While it's possible to reuse the getSavedPhotos method and just filter down to the requested ID, it's more elegant to have a function just for this purpose, and adding a method won't complicate things too much. Add a getSinglePhoto method to PhotosService:

```
ng2/rx-photos/src/app/photos.service.ts
getSinglePhoto(photoId) {
  return this.http.get<IPhoto>(this.api + '/getSinglePhoto/' + photoId);
}
```

Next, you need to tap into that new method. Open up edit-photo.component.ts and add the following (import as needed):

```
ng2/rx-photos/src/app/edit-photo/edit-photo.component.ts
constructor(
❶  private currentRoute: ActivatedRoute,
❷  private photosService: PhotosService
) {}
```

❶ Injecting an ActivatedRoute results in an object that represents the current route. We'll use this to grab information about the route itself.

❷ This is the photo service created earlier. In this case, we'll use it to fetch a single photo, rather than make a search.

Once everything's injected, it's time to figure out what photo the user wants to edit. The currentRoute object has a property paramMap—an observable that returns the latest details about the route parameters we defined in the route definition. Since this is an observable, rather than a fixed set of properties, Angular can handle changes to the route parameters without reloading the entire component. The application runs faster and our users are happy. Everyone wins!

Whenever the photoId in the route params changes, we want to load details about that photo. If the params change before the previous details have finished loading, Rx should ditch the previous request and only focus on the current one. This is the job of switchMap, first discussed in *Advanced Async*. You'll need to import switchMap and ParamMap, as well as declare the photo$ property on the EditPhotoComponent class.

```
ng2/rx-photos/src/app/edit-photo/edit-photo.component.ts
ngOnInit() {
  this.photo$ = this.currentRoute.paramMap
    .pipe(
      switchMap((params: ParamMap) =>
        this.photosService.getSinglePhoto(params.get('photoId'))
      )
    );
}
```

None of this triggers until the UI actually cares about the results. To handle that, we'll unwrap the observable with the async pipe. However, quite a few elements on this page will need the information that's passed through photo$.

If each element adds an `async` pipe, that means a new subscription (and therefore, a new request) each time. Fortunately, Angular provides a solution to that problem: the *ngIf directive.

Using ngIf

Sometimes, we want to hold off on rendering a section of a page until something has finished loading. In this case, the entire page depends on the photo details being available. ngIf is a directive that can be attached to an element that only inserts that element (and all of its children) into the DOM after the condition passed to it evaluates to true. It will remove the element if the condition ever becomes false again (and so on). In our case, the condition starts at false and only moves to true once.

Add an *ngIf to the page that encompasses everything that wants to use the latest photo data. This prevents the page from trying to render before it's ready. Using as aliases the result of the photo$ observable, making it available as a variable to every child element without requiring that each element use the async pipe. The square brackets around the src attribute tell Angular to take whatever value is passed in (in this case, the URL of the photo) and set it as the src attribute:

```
<div *ngIf="photo$ | async as photo">
  <div class="row">
    <div class="col-xs-2 col-xs-offset-5">
      <img class="photo-detail img-rounded" [src]="photo.url">
    </div>
  </div>
</div>
```

Now that the page loads the photo details correctly, it's time to add interactivity with a simplified tag manager.

Tagging and Saving Photos

Time to add some interactivity to the page. Using as to alias photo only scopes that variable to the view. Not to worry, this is a standard pattern in Angular: load something page-wide with as, then pass that into methods on the component whenever you want to do something with that value.

Speaking of methods, it's time to add tagging to the edit page. In the view, a few div elements are using Bootstrap classes to keep things centered and looking nice. The key attribute here is [(ngModel)]="tagInput". The ngModel attribute is a special attribute provided by Angular that matches the value of an element on the page with the value contained by a property of the component. Much like the src attribute from before, the square brackets indicate that whatever value is contained by the tagInput property of our component is also bound to the element itself. The parens work in the opposite direction—as the value of the input element changes, so does the component's value. Clicking the "Add Tag" button at the end calls the addTag method on the component (which you'll add right after this). The value of photo is passed through.

ng2/rx-photos/src/app/edit-photo/edit-photo.component.html
```html
<div class="row">
  <div class="col-xs-4 col-xs-offset-4">
    <div class="input-group">
      <input [(ngModel)]="tagInput" type="text" class="form-control"
        placeholder="Input Tag">
      <span class="input-group-btn">
        <button class="btn btn-default" type="button"
          (click)="addTag(photo)">Add Tag</button>
      </span>
    </div>
  </div>
</div>
```

The addTag method is nothing surprising. It just adds a tag to the photo object passed in, and resets the form. Changing the value of the component's property lets Angular know that we also want to change the value on the page itself through the square brackets on ngModel.

ng2/rx-photos/src/app/edit-photo/edit-photo.component.ts
```typescript
addTag(photo: IPhoto) {
  photo.tags.push(this.tagInput);
  this.tagInput = '';
}
```

Now that the user can add tags, we need to display them on the page. You'll use *ngIf again to prevent displaying the tag list before there are any tags to show, and *ngFor to iterate over all of the tags that have been added so far.

ng2/rx-photos/src/app/edit-photo/edit-photo.component.html
```html
<div class="row" *ngIf="photo.tags.length">
  <div class="col-xs-4 col-xs-offset-4">
    Tags:
    <ul>
      <li *ngFor="let tag of photo.tags">{{ tag }}</li>
    </ul>
  </div>
</div>
```

After the user has added tags to their heart's delight, they need to save the photo. First, the photo service needs a new method that saves the details of a single photo:

```
ng2/rx-photos/src/app/photos.service.ts
savePhoto(photo: IPhoto) {
  return this.http.put(this.api + '/updatePhoto', photo);
}
```

Once that's in, add a button to the page to call the new method:

```
ng2/rx-photos/src/app/edit-photo/edit-photo.component.html
<div class="row">
  <div class="col-xs-4 col-xs-offset-4">
    <button class="btn btn-success"
      (click)="photos.savePhoto(photo)">Save</button>
  </div>
</div>
```

In this case, the view can call directly through to the service, because the function will only be called on every click event, not every time something changes.

There's one final change to make to this page. Right now, there's a new call to save a photo every time the user clicks the Save button, even when there's already an active request. There's now a saving property to the component. You've learned that you can bind that property to an attribute with square brackets. Bind the saving property to the disabled attribute of the Save button with [disabled]="saving". With this, the main functionality of your website is complete. Let's add some analytics to track how people use the site and plug in a universal HTTP error handler.

Adding in Analytics

Let's hook up some analytics trackers to Angular's router. Instead of listening in on individual routes, this service needs to know about every route change. Generate a new service and attach it to the routing module with ng g service analytics.

 Make sure you're on the latest version of the Angular CLI. Older versions will fail, with "Error: Specified module does not exist."

Open the fresh analytics.service.ts and modify it to add in some structure for recording routing changes:

ng2/rx-photos/src/app/analytics.service.ts
```
import { Injectable } from '@angular/core';

@Injectable({
  providedIn: 'root'
})
export class AnalyticsService {
  constructor() { }

  recordPageChange(event) {
    // Call your analytics library
    console.log('Route triggered', event.urlAfterRedirects);
  }
}
```

This service just logs any route change to the console. You can import any analytics tool to connect the external tool with Angular. The real excitement goes on in app.component.ts:

ng2/rx-photos/src/app/app.component.ts
```
export class AppComponent implements OnInit {
  title = 'app';

❶  constructor(private router: Router, private analytics: AnalyticsService) { }

  ngOnInit() {
❷    this.router.events
    .pipe(
❸      filter(event => event instanceof NavigationEnd)
    )
    .subscribe(event => {
❹      this.analytics.recordPageChange(event);
    });
  }
}
```

❶ AppComponent now requires injecting both the Router and the newly created AnalyticsService. Don't forget to import these.

❷ As covered before, router.events is an observable that emits on any event the router might care to send off.

❸ The analytics code only cares about recording page loads, so we filter out any emitted event that isn't an instance of NavigationEnd.

❹ Finally, inform the analytics code that there's been a new page change.

There are other events to listen in for, but this serves as a simple example for capturing events on the router. Angular's RxJS integration also lets you intercept and modify AJAX calls through HttpClient.

Intercepting HTTP Calls

In addition to return types and JSON parsing, HttpClient introduces *interceptors*—a tool that exposes any AJAX request made in the application for modification. Let's add two of these. One, a conditional retry service, attempts to intelligently rerun failed HTTP requests behind the scenes before the user sees an error state and manually retries. The other listens in to every request and on an unreconcilable error, cleanly displays an error message (as opposed to a flow-breaking alert or a silent failure).

The first step to building an interceptor is to generate a service to hold that structure. Generate a new service with ng g service retry-interceptor and open it. Modify it to add the following:

```
import { Injectable } from '@angular/core';
import { Observable } from 'rxjs';
import {
  HttpResponse,
  HttpErrorResponse,
  HttpEvent,
  HttpInterceptor,
  HttpRequest,
  HttpHandler
} from '@angular/common/http';

@Injectable({
  providedIn: 'root'
})
export class RetryInterceptorService implements HttpInterceptor {

  constructor() { }

  intercept(request: HttpRequest<any>, next: HttpHandler):
    Observable<HttpEvent<any>> {
  }
}
```

❶ There are a lot of imports from HTTP here, but don't worry about understanding all of them at this point.

❷ The HttpInterceptor interface is what tells Angular about the role of this service—you'll see it come into play later in this section.

❸ The meat of an interceptor service is in the well-named intercept method. The first parameter, request, is an immutable object containing details about the request itself. To modify the actual request, you'd use the clone method. The next parameter is a tool that lets us run the rest of the interceptors and finally sends the full request.

In this case, the interceptor is concerned with what happens *after* the request is sent off, so the body of intercept needs to pass off the request to next.handle before it does anything. Fill in the body of intercept with the following:

```
ng2/rx-photos/src/app/retry-interceptor.service.ts
return next.handle(request)
.pipe(
  retryWhen(err$ =>
    err$
    .pipe(
      flatMap(err => {
        if (err instanceof HttpErrorResponse
          && err.status < 600 && err.status > 499) {
          return of(null)
            .pipe(delay(500));
        }
        return throwError(err);
      })
    )
  )
);
```

❶ If the request failed with a 5xx error, we return an observable of nothing to indicate that the request should be retried.

❷ Before it retries, the inner observable adds a delay of 500 ms to ensure the server doesn't get overloaded with multiple simultaneous retries.

❸ In the case of any other error, the inner observable rethrows the error so that later on, error handlers are aware of what's happening.

The RetryInterceptor could just use the retry operator from *Managing Asynchronous Events*, but that would mean retrying every non-2xx request, including the 4xx class of errors where no amount of retrying will fix the problem, or worse, retrying when there's an unrecoverable syntax error. Instead, we use retryWhen, which allows us to handle the error as an observable stream, optionally retrying after a check to ensure the status code is in the 500 class. The retryWhen operator merrily passes along values unmodified until the parent observable emits an error event. In that case, retryWhen emits a regular next event to the inner observable, containing the error. If the inner observable throws an error, then no retry happens.

Now that the interceptor is built out, you need to register it with its parent module. HttpInterceptors are special cases. Open up app.module.ts and update your providers array with the new object (PhotosService should already be there). The special HTTP_INTERCEPTORS provider informs Angular that this isn't just any old service, but rather one that has a specific purpose listening in to HTTP calls.

```
ng2/rx-photos/src/app/app.module.ts
providers: [
  {
    provide: HTTP_INTERCEPTORS,
    useClass: RetryInterceptorService,
    multi: true
  }
],
```

This interceptor can attempt to retry a few times, but at some point, it's time to admit defeat and inform the user that the request has failed. Run ng g service failure-interceptor and fill it out the same way you did with the RetryInterceptor. We use the tap operator here to tap into the returned request. Like subscribe, tap also optionally takes a Subscriber, so we can use the same trick as the save photo method. Many things can go wrong, so our method checks to ensure that the error actually has to do with AJAX before it displays the error.

```
return next.handle(request).do({
  error: (err: any) => {
  if (err instanceof HttpErrorResponse) {
    let msg = `${err.status}: ${err.message}`;
    this.errorService.showError(msg);
  }
});
```

What We Learned

This was your first look into how RxJS can be integrated into a larger framework. You learned about how RxJS can be used to pass AJAX calls around in an application, as well as to hook into the router of a single-page app. Angular services powered by RxJS can allow your application to query and update information without using up lots of extraneous resources.

There's more to learn about how RxJS turbocharges web frameworks. In the next chapter, you'll learn about using reactive forms to simplify many of your woes around building web forms.

If you want to dig further into the Angular world, you can add a few more features to this project. First, check out the [routerLinkActive] directive to make it clearer to the user which page they're on. This directive lets you add a class to a link element if the current page is the one the element links to. Some more features to stretch your newfound angular skills are to: create a universal error handler for all observables, show in the UI when a photo in the results page has already been saved, and add the ability to remove an already saved photo.

CHAPTER 7

Building Reactive Forms in Angular

Initially defined in 1999, the <form> element has powered the web ever since. Web forms started out as an obtuse collection of inputs that only validated when the user submitted the entire form, resetting everything if one detail was off. In the modern era, our users expect much more from forms. Our forms need to load quickly, respond with inline validation, and save the user's state so nothing is lost due to a connection hiccup or page refresh. Angular sprinkles RxJS liberally across its form tooling with the ReactiveForms module, bringing a decades-old element up to the cutting edge.

This chapter walks you through creating a set of forms for a pizza shop, showcasing the many features of reactive forms along the way. At first, the focus will be on a single input element, slowly composing in more functionality until you've created an impressively functional set of web forms, all built on an observable backbone.

Building a Phone Number Input

Of all the form inputs that have been written over the years, the phone number input box stands out as one of the most deceptively complex. On the surface, it appears simple—everyone knows what a phone number is! Underneath the surface, things get more complicated. There are many wrong ways to build a phone number input. A form could expect a specific format of phone number, rejecting everything else, but fail to let the user know which format it expects. Should there be parentheses around the area code? What about the country code? Even the biggest fan of your software will run screaming to a competitor if the form insists on (entirely hidden) formatting rules as shown in the screenshot on page 100.

Phone Number:	123-456-7890
Phone Number:	1234567890
Phone Number:	+1 123-456-7890
Phone Number:	(123) 456-7890

The other side of the coin is form elements that do way too much parsing. This unhelpful input box sliced off anything after the first nine characters (and worse, didn't validate anything):

	Browser autofill inputs (123) 456-7890
Phone Number:	(123) 456

Worst of all are forms that ask for a phone number but don't need one in the first place. Take a moment to consider: does this form really need a phone number input, or is it there just because everyone else does it? Even a fancy library like RxJS won't save you from building functionality you never needed in the first place.

The Right Way

Now, how would we build a phone number input the *right* way? A good form input should:

- Clearly show what sort of format is recommended.

- Accept all kinds of formats, regardless of whether they're pasted, typed, or entered through the browser's autofill tool.

- Reformat the phone number in an easy-to-read way if possible.

- Clearly indicate problems when they occur and what needs to be done to fix them.

This is possible using just techniques from the first section of this book.

```
fromEvent('blur', myInput)
.pipe(
  pluck('target', 'value'),
  map(phoneNumber => phoneNumber.replace(/[^\d]*/g, '')),
  filter(phoneNumber => phoneNumber.length === 10),
// ...etc
```

While you could build out a large form to this spec using RxJS alone, managing all of the elements would get complicated quickly. Thankfully, Angular has an answer to make building useful forms easier than ever. Angular supports two types of forms: Template forms and Reactive forms. Template forms use the same concepts from AngularJS where each form element is manually assigned a property and managed independently (though you don't need AngularJS knowledge to use them).

Modifying applications with template forms can be problematic—I've taken down a service because I added a form element in the view and never connected it to the JavaScript object that represented the state of the form. This meant that the value sent to the server was invalid, and the backend rejected all changes. Whoops.

The engineers who built Angular's reactive forms knew about the fragility of the old ways, and now all roads lead to a single source of truth for the form definition, in both the model and the view. Without further ado, it's time to start building your own phone number input.

Adding Reactive Forms

It's time to start coding. Generate a new application with the ng CLI tool you installed in *Using HTTP in Angular*.

```
ng new rx-pizza --routing
```

This application uses Bootstrap's CSS to give things a modicum of visual appeal. Open index.html and bring in the CSS: add the following tag to the <head> of the file (don't forget to have the book server running in addition to the ng serve call):

```
ng2/pizza/src/index.html
<!-- Bootstrap (loaded from local server) -->
<link rel="stylesheet" href="http://localhost:3000/assets/bootstrap.min.css">
```

Some placeholder HTML is generated in app.component.html. Remove everything and replace it with:

```
ng2/pizza/src/app/app.component.html
<div class="container">
  <router-outlet></router-outlet>
</div>
```

Reactive forms are not included by default with Angular, so the first thing to do is import them at the application level. While it's possible to use both template-driven and reactive forms in the same application, they diverge dramatically in both concepts and implementation details. I do not recommend that you mix the two. Open app.module.ts and add the following lines:

```
import { BrowserModule } from '@angular/platform-browser';
import { NgModule } from '@angular/core';

import { AppRoutingModule } from './app-routing.module';
import { AppComponent } from './app.component';
import { ReactiveFormsModule } from '@angular/forms';

/* ... snip ... */
@NgModule({
  imports: [
    BrowserModule,
    AppRoutingModule,
    ReactiveFormsModule
  ],
  declarations: [
    AppComponent
  ],
  bootstrap: [ AppComponent ]
})
export class AppModule { }
```

❶ The ReactiveFormsModule is imported from @angular/forms, a package that also contains the code for template-driven forms. The Angular compiler is smart enough to include only the code you need, so this import won't bring in the code for template-driven forms.

❷ Adding to the imports property at the root level ensures that the tools in ReactiveFormsModule will be available throughout the applications.

> **Joe asks:**
> ## Why Do I Need to Import Form Tools?
>
> Angular does not include any tooling for working with forms by default and instead requires the developer to manually import them (either template or reactive). Angular is designed this way to keep build sizes down. In AngularJS, all of the tooling for working with forms was included, even if the application didn't use all of it. Every time the user loaded a page, lots of superfluous code would be downloaded and parsed, slowing things down. With Angular, you have to explicitly ask for such tools to be included, resulting in a code bundle that only includes what's used.

Now that the application's components can access all the tools from the Reactive Forms module, it's time to generate a new component. Create a new component with ng generate component phone-num and add a declaration to the routing module like you did in *Using HTTP in Angular*. Start the Angular server with ng serve, and make sure you can navigate to the phone num component. Add a route to app-routing.module.ts for this new component:

ng2/pizza/src/app/app-routing.module.ts
```
{
  path: 'phone',
  component: PhoneNumComponent
},
```

Now that the boilerplate is out of the way, let's construct the component itself.

Creating a Phone Input with Angular

This component will house all of the tooling for the first iterations of our phone number input. Open phone-num.component.ts and import FormControl and Abstract-Control:

ng2/pizza/src/app/phone-num/phone-num.component.ts
```
import { FormControl, AbstractControl } from '@angular/forms';
```

FormControl is the root building block of all reactive forms in Angular. It represents a single input on the page. FormControl objects can be combined together into larger collections of elements, but for now let's focus on just getting the phone number input working. Used when validating inputs, AbstractControl is a type definition that defines what properties and methods you can access. (AbstractControl covers not only FormControl objects, but also FormGroup and FormArray, which you'll learn about later in this chapter.) The next step is to create a FormControl property on our controller. Add the following line as a declaration to the PhoneNumComponent class:

```
export class PhoneNumComponent implements OnInit {
  phoneNumber = new FormControl();

<div class="row">
  <div class="col-xs-2">
    <label for="phoneNum">Phone Number:</label>
  </div>
  <div class="col-xs-10">
    <input [formControl]="phoneNumber" class="form-control" id="phoneNum"/>
  </div>
</div>
```

Most of the HTML is styling. The important part to look at is <input [formControl]="phoneNumber"/>. This input uses the Angular directive formControl to connect that input to the phoneNumber FormControl property on our component. Changes to this input are reflected in the value of this.phoneNumber.value. So far, so standard. Let's take a peek behind the curtain to inspect what tooling reactive forms unlocks for us.

Validating an Input

The FormControl constructor has three optional parameters. The first is a default value for the form element. The type of this parameter is also used to inform Angular about what sort of form element to expect to be attached to this FormControl. The second and third parameters are arrays that contain the synchronous and asynchronous validation logic, respectively, for this individual element. Each validation rule is a function that is given the form control element (this is where we use the AbstractControl that was imported earlier) and then returns either null, if there's no error, or an object containing details about what's gone wrong. Let's take a look at how we might implement a validator for the phone number.

Built-In Validators

 In this section, you'll build your own validator, but it's important to remember that Angular comes with a handful of pre-written validators. You'll learn about those in the next section.

It's possible to ignore all three parameters, and Angular will default to a text input with no validation. We want some validation to ensure that the user gives us a valid phone number. In this case, all of the validation can be done synchronously—there's no need to ask a server for extra validation help, so the third parameter is unnecessary. We'll have a single, synchronous validation rule that ensures the user has entered a ten-digit number.

ng2/pizza/src/app/phone-num/phone-num.component.ts
```
export class PhoneNumComponent implements OnInit {
  phoneNumber = new FormControl('', [
    (control: AbstractControl) => {
      // remove anything that isn't a digit
      const numDigits = control.value.replace(/[^\d]+/g, '').length;
      // Only worried about US-based numbers for now, no need for country code
      if (numDigits === 10) { return null; }
      // Uh oh, something's wrong
      if (numDigits > 10) {
        return {
          tooLong: { numDigits }
        };
      } else {
        return {
          tooShort: { numDigits }
        };
      }
    }
  ]);
```

When the phone number is valid, the validator function returns null to indicate that there's no error. When there is an error, a validator function returns an object. The keys of the object will be put on the keys of the error property of the formControl. If phoneNum.errors is falsy, you know the input is valid. Otherwise, there's an object with a key for each error. The values on the error object can be any information that would aid in debugging, or just true if there's nothing more to be said.

In this case, we include the current length, so the user knows whether they need to add more digits or they pressed a key one too many times. The convention is to attach relevant information to the validator, but have the full error message on the page to make it easier to translate into other languages. Now that we're validating our phone number object, we need to update the view to display this new information.

```
ng2/pizza/src/app/phone-num/phone-num.component.html
<input [formControl]="phoneNumber" />

<div *ngIf="phoneNumber.invalid">

  <div *ngIf="(phoneNumber.dirty || phoneNumber.touched)">

    <div *ngIf="phoneNumber.errors.tooLong">
      There's too many digits in your phone number!
      You entered {{ phoneNumber.errors.tooLong.numDigits }}
        digits (required: 10)
    </div>
    <div *ngIf="phoneNumber.errors.tooShort">
      Your phone number is too short!
      You entered {{ phoneNumber.errors.tooShort.numDigits }}
        digits (required: 10)
    </div>
  </div>
</div>
</div>
```

❶ You'll notice that these errors are gated off by an *ngIf statement. Angular throws property access errors if errors is undefined (that is, the input is correct), and we try to access the tooLong property (as opposed to AngularJS, which silently swallowed those errors). To avoid throwing errors when the element is correct, we check the invalid property, which will be true if there are any errors in validating phoneNumber.

❷ The two if statements have been separated for clarity. The second if statement, (phoneNumber.dirty || phoneNumber.touched) is a little more complicated. No one likes validation errors before they've even started, so this snippet only displays errors *after* the phoneNumber input has been selected or changed. The dirty state indicates that the input has changed from the original value—the user has input some value. The touched state is true if the user has focused on the form element. We need to check both, because sometimes automatic form fillers change an input without triggering the touched state (the input is dirty but not touched), or the user might highlight the input without changing anything (the input is touched but not dirty). You can listen in to these changes through phoneNumber.valueChanges, an observable of value changes.

❸ Once the outermost *ngIf is satisfied, it's time to tell the user what went wrong. Rather than a vague message of, "There were errors in submitting your form," at the end of the form, the user now has immediate, inline feedback as to what they've done wrong.

Finally, Angular will add classes to an input according to the state of that input. These classes are:[1]

State	If True	If False
The control has been visited.	ng-touched	ng-untouched
The control's value has changed.	ng-dirty	ng-pristine
The control's value is valid.	ng-valid	ng-invalid

You can add styling details to these CSS classes to add visual cues to help the user figure out what's valid and what's not. In the general validation case, we want to alert the user when they've changed an input (.ng-dirty) and it's not valid (.ng-invalid). Add these styles to styles.css:

ng2/pizza/src/styles.css
```
.ng-invalid.ng-dirty {
  border-color: #a94442;
  -webkit-box-shadow: inset 0 1px 1px rgba(0,0,0,.075);
  box-shadow: inset 0 1px 1px rgba(0,0,0,.075);
}
```

We were able to build out all of this with minimal code, and the criteria for a valid input is clear to both the engineer looking at the code and the user filling out the form. Bravo! Now, let's build out a full registration form.

Building a Pizzeria Registration Form

A single phone number isn't much use on its own. We need context about that number—whose number is it? Why should we send them a text message? In this section , you've been hired by your local pizza place to build out an

---

1. https://angular.io/guide/forms

Interactive Online Pizza Experience, that is, some forms, so that locals can order pizza without that awful hassle of talking to someone on the phone. The first full form you'll create is the registration form where users create their accounts. Practically speaking, we'll need their name, a password, phone number (to alert them when the pizza's about to arrive), address, and credit card details. First things first, run ng generate component registration-form and add a route for this new component:

ng2/pizza/src/app/app-routing.module.ts
```
{
  path: 'registration',
  component: RegistrationFormComponent
},
```

When the user has registered, we can store that information and fill in a large portion of the pizza order form you'll build later in this chapter. The first option that comes to mind is manually building out the registration form by creating a FormControl property for each input element in the form:

```
username = new FormControl('', /* validators */);
phoneNumber = new FormControl('', /* validators */);
streetAddress0 = new FormControl('', /* validators */);
streetAddress1 = new FormControl('', /* validators */);
city = new FormControl('', /* validators */);
/* etc, etc */
```

If you're already falling asleep, I don't blame you. Angular was supposed to save us from all this tedious copy/pasting! FormControl is the basic building block of reactive forms, but there are two abstractions that combine those building blocks into something much easier to work with. These controls can be collected into an object through FormGroup or an array with FormArray. For now, we'll focus on FormGroup, because it'll be used in virtually every reactive form you build. A FormGroup takes an object, where the keys are the names of the form elements and the values are FormControl objects.

```
myForm = new FormGroup({
  username: new FormControl('', /* validators */),
  phoneNumber: new FormControl('', /* validators */),
  /* etc */
})
```

This isn't much better. There's still the tedious creation of piles of FormControl objects. Here's the secret—you should never construct FormControl objects directly like this. Instead, import Angular's FormBuilder tool and let that do the heavy lifting. FormBuilder is smart enough to know what's being passed in, allowing you to skip the many redundant new FormControl constructors.

```
class RegistrationFormComponent implements OnInit {
  registrationForm: FormGroup;
  constructor(private fb: FormBuilder) {}

  onInit() {
    this.registrationForm = this.fb.group({
      username: ['', /* validators */],
      phoneNumber: ['', /* validators */]
    });
  }
}
```

Using FormBuilder results in much cleaner and less bloated codebases. Now we can create the form and only focus on the parts we care about (names, values, and validation), while still gaining access to all the tooling we saw in the earlier phone number example. Now that our component has a FormGroup, we need to update the view to connect it to the group as a whole, instead of sewing each individual component on.

```
<form [formGroup]="registrationForm">
  <label>
    Name:
    <input formControlName="username" />
  </label>
  <label>
    Phone Number:
    <input formControlName="phoneNumber" />
  </label>
  <div *ngIf="registrationForm.get('phoneNumber').invalid
    && (registrationForm.get('phoneNumber').dirty
      || registrationForm.get('phoneNumber').touched)">
    <div *ngIf="registrationForm.get('phoneNumber').errors.tooLong">
      There are too many digits in your phone number!
      Wanted 10, but you have
      {{ registrationForm.get('phoneNumber').errors.tooLong.numDigits }}
    </div>
    <div *ngIf="registrationForm.get('phoneNumber').errors.tooShort">
      Your phone number is too short!
      Wanted 10, but you have
      {{ registrationForm.get('phoneNumber').errors.tooShort.numDigits }}
    </div>
  </div>
</form>
```

There are a few small changes to note in the phone number snippet above to accomodate the fact that each input element is part of a larger form. First, everything's enclosed in a <form> tag. We've bound registrationForm to this tag using the formGroup directive. This clues in Angular to what this form is specifically looking for. If we introduce an input element that's not bound to a property on registrationForm, Angular will throw an error, alerting us to this mistake.

Now that we need to pluck the phoneNumber element off the form, rather than having the variable available in the view, the error section has become more verbose. Angular provides a getter here to avoid naming conflicts with properties already on registrationForm. Other than the new getter routine, this section of the form hasn't changed.

If the extensive getter routine is too cumbersome and clutters up your view, a solution is to add a get property to the component itself:

Getters and Setters

 Sometimes, you want the ease of using an object property, but whatever value will be stored there, can't be easily set. JavaScript provides the get and set keywords for this use case. This means that whenever the username or phoneNumber properties of the class are accessed, the getter function will be called, and the value of the property will be whatever the getter function returns. In this case, it's merely syntactic sugar, but it can also be useful for computed properties or ensuring a property stays within certain bounds.

ng2/pizza/src/app/registration-form/registration-form.component.ts

```
get username() { return this.registrationForm.get('username'); }
get phoneNumber() { return this.registrationForm.get('phoneNumber'); }

<div *ngIf="phoneNumber.invalid && (phoneNumber.dirty || phoneNumber.touched)">
  <div *ngIf="phoneNumber.errors.tooLong">
    There's too many digits in your phone number!
    Wanted 10 but you've got {{ phoneNumber.errors.tooLong.numDigits }}
  </div>
  <div *ngIf="phoneNumber.errors.tooShort">
    Your phone number is too short!
    Wanted 10 but you've got {{ phoneNumber.errors.tooShort.numDigits }}
  </div>
</div>
```

So far, so good on creating FormGroups to organize all of the various parts of our form. Now, let's dig further into the validation rules to see how they can assist us with our form.

Using Advanced Validation

Form validation is more than just ensuring the user entered something into each element. It can be a crucial asset for users on phones (where a contextual keyboard will pop up on the phone), folks who use screen readers, or people who are just in a hurry and don't notice minor mistakes. In all of these cases, having the form pop up reminders, as soon as it knows what's wrong, will be a boon for the user. Let's dive into validation beyond a basic phone number and brainstorm a few rules about our form.

Inline Error Messages

 For the remainder of this chapter, I'll skip adding the error messages to the form to keep focus on the topic of the section. The CSS you added in the previous section still applies here, so you can easily tell whether an input is invalid or not.

Validating Account Information

The first section of the form involves all the basic account information (username, email, phone, password). You could probably write out all the rules for this form in your sleep, but why do that, when we can just borrow from the Angular team?

The first element in the form is the username. There'll be the standard set of validations for any username—a minimum and maximum length, a character whitelist, and an asynchronous validator ensuring the username hasn't been taken yet. If you want to ensure this async functionality works, the three usernames already in the system are rkoutnik, taken, anotheruser.

```
ng2/pizza/src/app/registration-form/registration-form.component.ts
username: ['', [
  Validators.required,
  Validators.maxLength(20),
  Validators.minLength(5)
],
  [(control) => {
    return this.http.get(this.endpoint + 'reactiveForms/usernameCheck/'
      + control.value)
    .pipe(
      map((res: any) => {
        if (res.taken) {
          return { usernameTaken: true };
        }
      })
    );
  }]
],
```

The next item, email, is so standard that Angular has a built-in validator:

```
ng2/pizza/src/app/registration-form/registration-form.component.ts
email: ['', [
  Validators.required,
  Validators.email
]],
```

There's no built-in tool for validating a phone number, but we can use Valida-
tors.pattern to ensure our element passes a regex test. In this case we're just
checking for a valid U.S. phone number with the pattern of 123-456-7890 for
simplicity, as more complicated regexes are outside the scope of this book.
For bonus points, reuse the phone number validator you wrote in the previous
section.

```
ng2/pizza/src/app/registration-form/registration-form.component.ts
phoneNumber: ['', [
  Validators.required,
  Validators.pattern(/^[1-9]\d{2}-\d{3}-\d{4}/)
]],
```

The final pair of items in the signup form asks for a password and confirmation
of that password. This is the first time in form validation that we've had to
consider the state of the form outside of an individual element. First, we need
to ensure the password meets our length and complexity requirements.

```
ng2/pizza/src/app/registration-form/registration-form.component.ts
password: ['', [
  Validators.required,
  Validators.minLength(12),
  (ac: AbstractControl) => {
    const currentVal: string = ac.value;
    // Password must contain at least three of the four options
    // Uppercase, lowercase, number, special symbol
    let matches = 0;
    if (currentVal.match(/[A-Z]+/)) {
      matches++;
    }
    if (currentVal.match(/[a-z]+/)) {
      matches++;
    }
    if (currentVal.match(/\d+/)) {
      matches++;
    }
    if (currentVal.replace(/[A-Za-z0-9]/g, '')) {
      matches++;
    }
    if (matches < 3) {
      return { passwordComplexityFailed: true };
    }
  }
```

```
  ]],
  confirmPassword: ['', [
    Validators.required
  ]],
```

If we want to add global validators to our form, we can't add them element-by-element. Instead, fb.group takes a second parameter, an object with two properties: validator and asyncValidator. This is where we add validation logic that requires checking multiple elements at once. Each value is a function that takes an abstract control representing the entire form.

ng2/pizza/src/app/registration-form/registration-form.component.ts
```
validator: (ac: AbstractControl) => {
  const pw = ac.get('password').value;
  const cpw = ac.get('confirmPassword').value;
  if (pw !== cpw) {
    ac.get('confirmPassword').setErrors({passwordMismatch: true});
  }
}
```

Validating an Address

The address section has two layers of validation. First, each item needs to have its own individual set of validators, but the address as a whole needs to be checked against the backend to ensure that it's a valid address. The individual validations are simple:

ng2/pizza/src/app/registration-form/registration-form.component.ts
```
const addressModel = {
  street: ['', Validators.required],
  apartment: [''],
  city: ['', Validators.required],
  state: ['', Validators.required],
  zip: ['', [
    Validators.required,
    Validators.pattern(/\d{5}/)
  ]]
};
```

The backend check assembles the current value of the entire form and checks it against the backend. Async validators only run when all of the synchronous validators pass, so we don't need to worry about sending a half-completed address to the backend. We also add in a debounceTime operator to keep the overall number of requests low.

ng2/pizza/src/app/registration-form/registration-form.component.ts
```
const checkAddress = (control: AbstractControl) => {
  const address = {
    street: control.get('street').value,
```

```
    apartment: control.get('apartment').value,
    city: control.get('city').value,
    state: control.get('state').value,
    zip: control.get('zip').value
  };
  return this.http.get(this.endpoint + 'reactiveForms/addressCheck/' + address)
  .pipe(
    debounceTime(333),
    map((res: any) => {
      if (!res.validAddress) {
        return { invalidAddress: true };
      }
    })
  );
};
```

Finally, the address subform is attached to the main registration form:

ng2/pizza/src/app/registration-form/registration-form.component.ts
```
addresses: this.fb.array([
  this.fb.group(addressModel, {
    asyncValidator: checkAddress
  })
]),
```

Validating a Credit Card

The credit card section contains our first bit of complicated, custom validation. All credit card numbers follow the Luhn algorithm[2] for validation, which works like so:

- Double the second digit from the right, and every other digit after that (working from right to left). If the result of the doubling is greater than nine, add the digits together.

- Take the sum of all the resulting digits.

- If the final result is divisible by 10, the credit card is valid.

While you can't ever be sure a card is valid without first checking it with your payment processor, simple checks like the Luhn algorithm help catch errors where a customer might have accidentally entered a typo.

ng2/pizza/src/app/registration-form/registration-form.component.ts
```
const ccModel = {
  cc: ['', [
    Validators.required,
    (ac: AbstractControl) => {
```

---

2. https://en.wikipedia.org/wiki/Luhn_algorithm

```
          // Convert string to array of digits
          const ccArr: number[] = ac.value.split('').map(digit => Number(digit));
          // double every other digit, starting from the right
          let shouldDouble = false;
          const sum = ccArr.reduceRight((accumulator, item) => {
            if (shouldDouble) {
              item = item * 2;
              // sum the digits, tens digit will always be one
              if (item > 9) {
                item = 1 + (item % 10);
              }
            }
            shouldDouble = !shouldDouble;
            return accumulator + item;
          }, 0);

          if (sum % 10 !== 0) {
            return { ccInvalid: true };
          }
        }
      }
    ]],
    cvc: ['', Validators.required],
    expirationMonth: ['', [
        Validators.required,
        Validators.min(1),
        Validators.max(12)
    ]],
    expirationYear: ['', [
      Validators.required,
      Validators.min((new Date()).getFullYear())
    ]]
};
```

This is only the penultimate step on our journey of creating a form group—the final step is to collect all of these requirements together into a data model for your form.

Connecting the Model to the View

At a certain abstract level, any form has a data model attached to it, describing the properties of the form and the values they contain. For most forms, the parts of this data model are scattered around the view, several JavaScript files, and sometimes even partially stored on the backend. Making changes to the form involves checking for conflicts at all layers. One little mistake, and now you've brought prod down (or worse, prod's still up but you're capturing the wrong data).

Reactive forms instead use the concept of a central, class-based data model. Everything in the form is routed through this model—even to the point of throwing errors when you try to modify properties that don't exist on the model (a huge and welcome change from JavaScript's typical stance of silently allowing such changes, leading to developers thinking everything's OK). Data models are based on plain old JavaScript objects. At its simplest, a model for the registration form would look like this:

```
{
  username: [''],
  phoneNumber: [''],
  password: [''],
  confirmPassword: [''],
  address: {
    street: [''],
    apartment: [''],
    city: [''],
    state: [''],
    zip: ['']
  },
  creditCard: {
    cc: [''],
    cvc: [''],
    expirationMonth: [''],
    expirationYear: ['']
  }
}
```

The entire form is defined in this one object, showing the requirements for each element and how subgroups relate to each other. Angular uses this definition to validate the view—if ever there's an input that attempts to connect to a property that doesn't exist in the model, you will get an error. You have already built most of the data model by building out the validators and nested formGroups. Now let's link that model to the view and add a way to save the whole thing.

First, we'll deliberately break the view to demonstrate how the validation provided by reactive forms can save us from ourselves. Update the registration-form.component.html to be a form element with one input. [formGroup]="registrationForm" will hook up the form to the form element. The input is given a form control that doesn't exist on registrationForm:

```
<form [formGroup]="registrationForm">
  <input formControlName="notReal">
</form>
```

If your editor's smart enough, it might catch the error here. If not, open the page, and the console should have something like the screenshot on page 116.

```
ERROR Error: Cannot find control with name: 'notReal'
    at _throwError (forms.es5.js:1918)
    at setUpControl (forms.es5.js:1826)
    at FormGroupDirective.webpackJsonp.../../../forms/@angular/forms.es5.js.FormGroupDirective.addControl (forms.es5.js:4809)
    at FormControlName.webpackJsonp.../../../forms/@angular/forms.es5.js.FormControlName._setUpControl (forms.es5.js:5397)
    at FormControlName.webpackJsonp.../../../forms/@angular/forms.es5.js.FormControlName.ngOnChanges (forms.es5.js:5315)
    at checkAndUpdateDirectiveInline (core.es5.js:10853)
    at checkAndUpdateNodeInline (core.es5.js:12364)
    at checkAndUpdateNode (core.es5.js:12303)
    at debugCheckAndUpdateNode (core.es5.js:13167)
    at debugCheckDirectivesFn (core.es5.js:13108)
```

Presto! Angular has already figured out there's an error with our form and alerted us. Now that we've proven that Angular's aware of when we do the *wrong* thing, let's fill out the rest of the form inputs. First is the section containing all the formControls that aren't part of a subgroup:

```html
<form [formGroup]="registrationForm">
  <label>Username:
    <input formControlName="username">
  </label>
  <label>Phone Number:
    <input formControlName="phoneNumber">
  </label>
  <label>Password:
    <input formControlName="password" type="password">
  </label>
  <label>Confirm Password:
    <input formControlName="confirmPassword" type="password">
  </label>
</form>
```

There is nothing terribly new here, but do not forget those type="password" attributes.

Next up is the address section. First, add a convenience helper to the controller to get the addresses attribute::

```
ng2/pizza/src/app/registration-form/registration-form.component.ts
get addresses() {
  return this.registrationForm.get('addresses') as FormArray;
}
addAddress() {
  this.addresses.push(this.fb.group(addressModel));
}
```

This addresses isn't a regular method. Rather, it defines what happens whenever anything tries to access the addresses property of this component. This is necessary because we want to pull the addresses property off of the registrationForm using the getter, but that getter returns an AbstractControl. To take full advantage of the type hinting provided by Angular, the as FormArray is required. After you add the as FormArray, the rest of the component and view can access the form array without any worry.

The address is a nested formGroup, so the view uses a nested <form> element to represent that. It's not connected by binding the [formGroup] property. Rather, the directive formGroupName is used to indicate that this form tag relates to a subgroup. Inside the form tag, you refer to each form control directly (no need to add address.whatever to each input):

```
<form [formGroup]="registrationForm">
  <!-- Previously-created inputs hidden -->
  <form formGroupName="address">
    <label>Street:
      <input formControlName="street">
    </label>
    <label>Apartment (optional):
      <input formControlName="apartment">
    </label>
    <label>City:
      <input formControlName="city">
    </label>
    <label>State:
      <input formControlName="state">
    </label>
    <label>Zip:
      <input formControlName="zip">
    </label>
  </form>
</form>
```

That's the address section settled. Use the same technique to repeat this process on your own for the credit card section, using the same technique.

At this point, we have a fully functional pizza signup form. Time to add some fancy features. First of all, this is a rather large form. If the user filled it out, then hit a network error upon submitting and need to refresh the page, they'd be pretty frustrated. Let's subscribe to all changes on the form and save them to localStorage. Add the following to the end of the ngOnInit call:

```
ng2/pizza/src/app/registration-form/registration-form.component.ts
this.registrationForm.valueChanges
.subscribe(newForm => {
  window.localStorage.registrationForm = JSON.stringify(newForm);
});
```

This snippet doesn't change anything from the user's perspective. Once the form's saved, we need to restore up to the previous state on component init. To do that, you need to know how to programatically modify a given form group.

Updating Form Groups

Any FormGroup object has two methods that let us update the value of the form in bulk: setValue and patchValue. Both take an object and update the value of the form to match the properties of that object. setValue is the stricter of the two—the object passed in must exactly map to the object *definition* passed into form builder (it does not need to be recreated as FormControls, however). For example:

```
let myForm = fb.group({
  name: '',
  favoriteFood: ''
});

// This fails, we need to also provide favoriteFood
myForm.setValue({ name: 'Randall' });

// This works
myForm.setValue({
  name: 'Randall',
  favoriteFood: 'pizza'
});
```

The patchValue method doesn't care if the object passed in matches the form's requirements. Properties that don't match are ignored. In general, if you want to update part of a form or use an object that has superfluous properties, go with patchValue. If you have a *representation* of the form, use the superior error-checking of setValue. In the localStorage case, we have a representation of the form, so we grab the latest from localStorage and update the form with setValue. This snippet goes right above the subscribe call you added earlier:

```
ng2/pizza/src/app/registration-form/registration-form.component.ts
if (window.localStorage.registrationForm) {
  this.registrationForm.setValue(
      JSON.parse(window.localStorage.registrationForm));
}
```

Fill out part of the form and refresh the page. The parts you filled out should still be there. The form will survive through any network disaster.

Submitting the Form

One last thing for this section—the user needs to be able to save the form (and clear out that saved state). Add a save method to the controller and an accompanying button to the view:

```
ng2/pizza/src/app/registration-form/registration-form.component.ts
save() {
  return this.http.post(this.endpoint + 'reactiveForms/user/save',
    this.registrationForm.value)
```

```
    .subscribe(
      next => window.localStorage.registrationForm = '',
      err => console.log(err),
      () => console.log('done')
    );
}
```

The save method looks at the invalid property of the form (there's also an accompanying valid property) and enables the button only when the form is fully valid, to prevent accidental submissions.

ng2/pizza/src/app/registration-form/registration-form.component.html

```
<button
  class="btn btn-default"
  (click)="save()"
  [disabled]="registrationForm.invalid"
>Save</button>
```

The save method also resets the locally saved form value only when the save is successful. However, if the form's invalid, the user won't be able to submit it until the problems are corrected.

Now that the main thrust of the form has been completed, you can add more advanced features, such as allowing the user to input an arbitrary number of addresses.

Handling Multiple Addresses

This form is all well and good for users who use exactly one credit card and never leave the house. If we want to expand our target market beyond such a select group, the form needs to accomodate multiple inputs. The tool we use for this is FormArray, which represents a collection of FormGroups. First, take the extracted address model definition:

ng2/pizza/src/app/registration-form/registration-form.component.ts

```
const addressModel = {
  street: ['', Validators.required],
  apartment: [''],
  city: ['', Validators.required],
  state: ['', Validators.required],
  zip: ['', [
    Validators.required,
    Validators.pattern(/\d{5}/)
  ]]
};
```

Then update the actual declaration of addressForm to build a formArray, with a default of a single address:

ng2/pizza/src/app/registration-form/registration-form.component.ts

```
addresses: this.fb.array([
  this.fb.group(addressModel, {
    asyncValidator: checkAddress
  })
]),
```

Now we need to figure out how to iterate over a formArray in the model. Coun-
terintuitively, the formArray actually isn't an array. To access the collection of
form controls, we use the controls property. Inside that iteration, we create a form
element for each item in the address collection. The form's formGroupName is set
by index, because each formGroup doesn't have a specific name.

ng2/pizza/src/app/registration-form/registration-form.component.html

```
<h3>Addresses</h3>
<div formArrayName="addresses" *ngFor="let addr of addresses.controls;
    let i = index">
  <form [formGroupName]="i">
    <div class="form-group">
      <label>Street:
        <input class="form-control" formControlName="street">
      </label>
    </div>
    <div class="form-group">
      <label>Apartment (optional):
        <input class="form-control" formControlName="apartment">
      </label>
    </div>
    <div class="form-group">
      <label>City:
        <input class="form-control" formControlName="city">
      </label>
    </div>
    <div class="form-group">
      <label>State:
        <input class="form-control" formControlName="state">
      </label>
    </div>
    <div class="form-group">
      <label>Zip:
        <input class="form-control" formControlName="zip">
      </label>
    </div>
    <button
      type="button"
      [disabled]="addresses.controls.length === 1"
      class="btn btn-default"
      (click)="addresses.removeAt(i)"
```

```
  >Remove</button>
  <hr>
 </form>
</div>
<button type="button" class="btn btn-default" (click)="addAddress()">
  Add Address</button>
```

The Remove button calls the handy method removeAt to remove whatever address is stored at that index. At least one address is required, so the button is disabled, unless there are multiple addresses already. The Add button will require us to modify the component class. Add another method to the component that creates a new (empty) address and adds it to the form group:

ng2/pizza/src/app/registration-form/registration-form.component.ts

```
get addresses() {
  return this.registrationForm.get('addresses') as FormArray;
}
addAddress() {
  this.addresses.push(this.fb.group(addressModel));
}
```

This method takes advantage of the getter defined earlier. In this case, it adds a new, empty address to the form. Unfortunately, FormBuilder is not built into FormArray's push method, so we need to convert the address model into a group before passing it in.

When these two methods have been added to the controller, your registration form is complete. Click through to make sure everything works. When you're satisfied with the registration form, it's time to dig into ordering a pizza.

Creating a Pizza Ordering Form

Now that users have an account set up, they need the ability to order an actual pizza. Unlike the registration form, the order form has several parts that need to interact with each other. RxPizza wants to sell specialty pizzas and allow for trivial one-click ordering. Different sizes and toppings will change the price as the user fills out the form. We'll need to subscribe to select parts of our form and update other values on the page (sound familiar?).

You're already chomping at the bit to build this, so start off by generating the component with ng g component pizza-order and add a route to the route module:

```
{
  path: 'pizza',
  component: PizzaOrderComponent
},
```

Let's move on to the data model.

Building a Pizza Model

The core data model for our pizza form is thankfully simpler than the registration form. Add it to the component you just generated.

ng2/pizza/src/app/pizza-order/pizza-order.component.ts

```
// FormBuild can be instantiated outside of a component
const _fb = new FormBuilder();
class Pizza {
  size = 'medium';
  toppings = _fb.group({
    pepperoni: false,
    ham: false,
    pineapple: false,
    chicken: false,
    hotSauce: false
  });
  cheese = 'mozzarella';
  // For specialty pizzas
  name = '';
}
```

Instead of a plain JavaScript object, this data model is represented as a class. With this class, you can easily create new instances of the model, which will come in handy when adding new pizzas to the form.

 Joe asks:

Why Are Toppings Stored as an Object?

One would expect toppings to be stored as an array—after all, they're a collection. However, the pizzaModel stores toppings as a key/value object. This may be a bit confusing on the JavaScript side of things, but once you take a look at the view, things start clearing up. Each topping is represented by a single true/false checkbox. We need to reference toppings directly, and it's easier to do that with an object than constantly iterating through an array.

This model can be included in the root form group for the component, along with form controls for the address and credit card. The form will allow users to order multiple pizzas, so that's represented by a FormArray.

ng2/pizza/src/app/pizza-order/pizza-order.component.ts

```
this.pizzaForm = this.fb.group({
  address: ['', Validators.required],
  creditCard: ['', Validators.required],
  pizzas: this.fb.array([this.fb.group(new Pizza())])
});
```

Creating the Pizza View

The pizzaModel is where the meat of this form exists (as well as the dough, tomato sauce, and other toppings). It's set up at the root as an array (who orders just one pizza?), so we'll clone the formArray work from the previous form:

```
ng2/pizza/src/app/pizza-order/pizza-order.component.ts
get pizzas(): FormArray {
  return this.pizzaForm.get('pizzas') as FormArray;
}

addPizza() {
  this.pizzas.push(this.fb.group(new Pizza()));
}
```

Now that the boilerplate is out of the way, it's time to start writing the HTML for this form. For the first step, insert the all-important headline and a form element linked to pizzaForm. Everything after this will go in the form element.

```
<h1>Pizza Order Form</h1>
<form [formGroup]="pizzaForm">
</form>
```

Now on to the most important part—the pizza! This section of the form will iterate over all of the pizzas stored in the form (you've already initialized it with a single, empty pizza object).

```
ng2/pizza/src/app/pizza-order/pizza-order.component.html
<div *ngFor="let pizza of pizzas.controls; let i = index"
    [formGroupName]="i">
  <!-- TODO: specials -->
  <h3>Make it a Special</h3>
  <button *ngFor="let s of specials" (click)="selectSpecial(i, s)">
    {{ s.name }}
  </button>
  <h3>Size:</h3>
  <label>
    Small
    <input formControlName="size" type="radio" value="small">
  </label>
  <label>
    Medium
    <input formControlName="size" type="radio" value="medium">
  </label>
  <label>
    Large
    <input formControlName="size" type="radio" value="large">
  </label>
```

```
        <h3>Toppings:</h3>
        <div formGroupName="toppings">
          <span *ngFor="let t of toppingNames">
            <label>
              {{ t }}
              <input type="checkbox" [formControlName]="t">
            </label>
          </span>
        </div>
        <button type="button" (click)="pizzas.removeAt(i)">
          Remove this Pizza</button>
        <hr>
      </div>
    </div>
    <button type="button" (click)="addPizza()">Add Pizza</button>
```

The root of this section iterates over all the pizza objects stored in the FormArray, creating a new subsection for each one. Inside are elements asking the user to select a size and toppings for their pizza. The attribute [formGroupName]="i" binds these select elements to an individual pizza.

Finally, a pair of buttons provide the option to add a new pizza or remove an existing one. These buttons work just like the buttons in the address section.

If your editor is smart enough, it may have noticed that something's missing. Otherwise, you'll see an error in the JavaScript console: toppingNames is used in the view, but can't be found. Add it as a property on the component class:

ng2/pizza/src/app/pizza-order/pizza-order.component.ts
```
toppingNames = [
  'pepperoni',
  'ham',
  'pineapple',
  'chicken',
  'hotSauce'
];
```

Now that basic pizza selection is handled, the next step is to add pickers for the address and credit card.

Fetching Component Data in the Route

The address and credit card inputs are simplified to just dropdowns in this example, filled in with data fetched from the server. While you could add a few ajax calls in the component itself, Angular's routing allows you to define the async data a component needs and load it alongside all of the other data that component needs. This can be used to gracefully handle errors and redirect as the component loads.

To fetch custom data during the routing, you need to create a special type of service called a Resolver. A resolver is just a fancy name for a service with a resolve method that gets called when Angular needs to route to a given page. Our resolve method will make two AJAX calls and return an observable of the resulting data. Generate a service with ng g service user-detail-resolver and fill in the details with the following:

```
ng2/pizza/src/app/user-detail-resolver.service.ts
import { Injectable } from '@angular/core';
import {
  Router, Resolve
} from '@angular/router';
import { combineLatest } from 'rxjs';
import { ajax } from 'rxjs/ajax';
import { pluck, map } from 'rxjs/operators';

@Injectable()
❶ export class UserDetailResolver implements Resolve<any> {
  constructor() { }

  resolve() {
    return combineLatest(
      ajax('http://localhost:3000/ng2/reactiveForms/userData/addresses')
      .pipe(pluck('response')),
      ajax('http://localhost:3000/ng2/reactiveForms/userData/creditCards')
      .pipe(pluck('response'))
    )
    .pipe(
      map(responses => {
        return {
          addresses: responses[0],
          creditCards: responses[1]
        };
      })
    );
  }
}
```

❶ The snippet implements Resolve<any> tells us two things. One, that this class is intended to be used any place a resolver should be (if it's used outside of the router, something's wrong). Second, the <any> can be used to indicate the type of data the resolver will return. In this case, it's not important, so any is used to declare that the resolver could return any type of data (or nothing at all).

Once that's done, you can create a route for the pizza ordering component and include the resolve parameter:

```
ng2/pizza/src/app/app-routing.module.ts
{
  path: 'pizza',
  component: PizzaOrderComponent,
  resolve: {
    userDetails: UserDetailResolver
  }
},
```

Finally, add private route: ActivatedRoute to the constructor of the pizza form component and listen in to the result of resolver in ngOnInit. You also need to add a userDetails: any to the top of the component class.

```
ng2/pizza/src/app/pizza-order/pizza-order.component.ts
this.route.data
.subscribe(data => {
  this.userDetails = data.userDetails;
});
```

Adding Reactive Selectors

Thankfully, dropdown selectors are as simple as can be with reactive forms. Bind to the form control as usual, and iterate over the data provided in userDetails to create an <option> element for each one.

```
ng2/pizza/src/app/pizza-order/pizza-order.component.html
<div>
  <h3>Payment</h3>
  <select formControlName="creditCard">
    <option *ngFor="let card of userDetails.creditCards" [ngValue]="card">
      {{ card }}
    </option>
  </select>
</div>
```

Use the same pattern to add an address selector to the form.

Reacting to Change

At some point, the customer needs to know how much all these pizzas will cost them. Observables let us react to user input to keep an updated total price on the page, but how do we recalculate the price only when relevant information is updated? We know the entire form can be subscribed to with .valueChanges—and that's what we'll use for the individual form controls as well. We can extract the properties of the form with this.pizzaForm.get(nameOfProperty).

We'll need an observable stream of all changes to pizzas, mapped through a function that calculates the total cost:

```
ng2/pizza/src/app/pizza-order/pizza-order.component.ts
this.price$ = this.pizzaForm.get('pizzas').valueChanges
.pipe(
  map((pizzaList: any[]) => pizzaList
    .reduce((total, pizza) => {
      let price;
      switch (pizza.size) {
        case 'small': price = 10; break;
        case 'medium': price = 14; break;
        case 'large': price = 19; break;
      }

      const numToppings = this.toppingNames
      .filter(x => pizza.toppings[x]).length;
      price += (numToppings * 0.5);
      return total + price;
    }, 0)
  )
);
```

Inside calculatePrice, we implement the cost logic, charging a base price for pizza size and adding $0.50 for each topping. Remember, toppings is an object, so we need to do a bit of fancy logic to determine just how many toppings the user has selected.

Now the form should display the latest price to the user using the async pipe you learned about before:

```
ng2/pizza/src/app/pizza-order/pizza-order.component.html
<div>
  <h3>Price: ${{ price$ | async }}</h3>
  <button type="button">Submit</button>
</div>
```

Specialty Pizzas

Now we have a relatively functional (if plain) order form. Time to zest that up with some specials. In our case, the specials will be pre-configured collections of toppings (nothing too crazy). This also let's the user customize the specials (maybe you're not a fan of hot sauce, but love everything else about buffalo chicken). The traditional form story doesn't provide much comfort here, but through patchValue, reactive forms make this easy.

First, let's set up two specials for today—Hawaiian and Buffalo Chicken. Add the following code as a property declaration on the component class:

```
ng2/pizza/src/app/pizza-order/pizza-order.component.ts
specials = [{
  name: 'Buffalo Chicken',
  toppings: {
    pepperoni: false,
    ham: false,
    pineapple: false,
    chicken: true,
    hotSauce: true
  }
}, {
  name: 'Hawaiian',
  toppings: {
    pepperoni: false,
    ham: true,
    pineapple: true,
    chicken: false,
    hotSauce: false
  }
}];
```

Both of these are partial models—that is, they define only part of a pizza model. A special shouldn't define the *size* of a pizza, so we'll leave that up to whatever the user chooses. The view is simple—just iterate over the specials and display a button for each. Add the following where the <!-- TODO: specials --> comment is:

```
<h3>Make it a Special</h3>
<button *ngFor="let s of specials" (click)="selectSpecial(i, s)">
  {{ s.name }}
</button>
```

The selectSpecial method is trivial to implement—it's just a wrapper around patchValue:

```
ng2/pizza/src/app/pizza-order/pizza-order.component.ts
selectSpecial(pizzaIndex, special) {
  this.pizzas.controls[pizzaIndex].patchValue(special);
}
```

What We Learned

Forms are one of the areas where Rx is most effective in simplifying common frontend tasks. This goes doubly so, when coupled with a framework like Angular to handle all of the intermediate connections for you. With these two tools combined, you're equipped to build powerful, easy-to-use forms without skimping on key features. Your forms can now include validation that's helpful, react quickly to user input, and involve seemingly complex controls.

There's still more that RxJS can do for you in the world of Angular. In this chapter, the form held all the state of the page. In the next chapter, you'll learn about ngrx, a centralized state management system that sits on top of RxJS, as well as using clever RxJS tricks to track and optimize the performance of an Angular web application.

If you're still hungry for more challenge after finishing the projects in this chapter, here's a few suggestions about how to expand the pizza forms.

Create Stricter Validation

While our registration form has fairly comprehensive validation rules, there are a few more corner cases you can tackle. How would you ensure that the expiration date entered for a credit card is in the future? How can you support more formats and types of phone numbers (hint: this might require more than a regex)?

Add More Items to Order

Pizza joints sell more than just pizza. How would you add soda, garlic bread, and similar items into the current form model? Would you use separate subforms like the pizzas or just another component? What would the form model look like?

New Specialty Pizzas

Not everyone thinks that pineapple and ham make a good pizza. How would you let a user create and customize their own specialty pizzas? Where would that be stored?

CHAPTER 8

Advanced Angular

Angular is a powerful framework, with many knobs and levers to tweak, if you know where to look. This chapter will act as your guide to all those hidden details you might otherwise miss. The first major topic is performance. Angular is a fast framework, but we can unintentionally create situations where pages drag to a halt, even on our shiny developer machines. You'll learn how to check for those performance issues and use Rx to work with the Angular framework to skip loads of unneeded operations. After that, you'll tackle one of the biggest challenges modern-day application developers face: state management. While Angular itself doesn't have a state management framework, members of Angular's core team maintain the ngrx library for that purpose, which is considered the de facto solution.

Building Performant Applications

A slow application is not a useful one. We developers can get complacent with our powerful machines and speedy fiber connections. We forget that most of the world connects through a phone, on a connection no better than 3G. Speed matters even more than ever—47% of users leave a page if it takes longer than 2 seconds to render.[1]

In this section, you'll learn how to profile an Angular application and use observables to skip large swaths of unneeded performance issues.

Understanding Angular Performance

There are two types of performance to think about when digging through any frontend application: load and runtime. Load performance focuses on how quickly the application can get up and running for the user. Runtime

---

1. https://blog.kissmetrics.com/loading-time/

performance is concerned with how quickly the application can respond to user input after it has loaded. While Angular provides many powerful tools to help optimize load performance (such as ahead-of-time compilation and service workers), these tools do not use observables and are outside the scope of this book. Angular's runtime performance tooling uses nothing but observables, so I'm sure you're ready to dive in.

Angular's runtime performance boils down to one question: When something happens on the page (a click event or an AJAX request returning), how quickly can Angular make sure that all the data stored in models and displayed on the page is the correct information? This process is known as Change Detection. Angular's predecessor, AngularJS, kept things simple by checking everything on every change. This ensured that no data would be stale, but created a hard limit for how much data could be checked before the web app started slowing down. Angular drastically changed things, optimizing both sides of the equation: when should I run change detection and what needs to be checked? The first half of the question was resolved with Zones.

Using Zones to Run Change Detection

Zones are a new concept to JavaScript, but they were a core language feature in Dart, a language Google created to replace JavaScript. Dart never gained traction, but zones made their way over to the JavaScript ecosystem to be a foundational part of Angular. In short, zones are a way to wrap asynchronous code into a single context. Let's say you wanted to figure out how long an AJAX call took with regard to code execution time on the frontend. Something like this wouldn't work:

```
startTimer();
ajax(url)
.pipe(
  map(result => processResult(result)
)
.subscribe(
  () => stopTimer()
);
```

The timer here would measure the entire scope of the request—the initiating code, the time spent waiting for the server to return the information, and the time spent processing the returned value. If the main thread is doing something at the moment the request returns, that is also tracked in the timer.

Instead, zones can wrap this call. A zone is only active when the code inside it is executing. Zones also allow us to write handlers that execute whenever the code contained within the zone begins or ends execution.

In Angular, these zones are used to wrap common frontend APIs like addEventListener and the XmlHTTPRequest object. This means Angular applications don't need to write convoluted wrappers to be aware of all click events. Instead, Angular creates a new zone for all click events, and anytime that zone finishes executing, Angular runs change detection to see what's been modified. Expand this to all events across an application, and Angular has a fine-grained idea of what's going on within your application without additional effort on your part.

While it's possible to create new zones, Angular sets up its own set of zones automatically, so you don't need to.

Escaping the Context

 Sometimes you might want to run something without triggering an entire change detection cycle. In this case, you'd need to run the code outside of Angular's zone, so you can inject NgZone and use NgZone.runOutsideAngular(someFunction) to modify things.

When Angular determines that a change detection cycle needs to be run, the next task is to determine just what needs to be checked. Angular stores the state in a tree model, starting with the app-level component that mirrors how each component is placed in the DOM. Using the default settings, Angular starts at that root component and checks the various properties on that component, updating the DOM along the way as needed. Each component has its own independent change detector that runs during this process.

Profiling Change Detection

Now that you know what's going on behind the scenes, let's tap into those flows to see how observables are used to run the change detection. While digging through Angular's internals, you'll build some tooling to track the length of each change detection cycle. I've created an application that has some performance issues for you to debug in the bad-perf directory. Start that up with ng serve and look at the resulting page.

This application is a patient processing system for a hospital (using fake data generated by Faker.js[2])—certainly a situation where page response time matters. Fire it up and browse through the (fictitious) patients. You'll notice that updating anything on the page takes a while. Certainly the page *feels* sluggish—but can we prove it?

Generate a new service with ng generate service cd-profiler. This service is in charge of tracking how long each change detection cycle takes and reporting it to

---

2. https://github.com/marak/Faker.js/

you. Everything is orchestrated through Angular's zone, NgZone, so the first order of business is to inject that into our service:

ng2/perf-complete/src/app/cd-profiler.service.ts
```
constructor(private zone: NgZone) {
```

NgZone provides two key observable streams: onUnstable, which signals the start of change detection and onStable, signaling the end. We want to listen in on each one of these, mapping the results to add details about what type of event happened and what time the event took place. Add the following to the constructor in the service you just generated.

ng2/perf-complete/src/app/cd-profiler.service.ts
```
const unstableLatest$ = zone.onUnstable
.pipe(
  map(() => {
    return {
      type: 'unstable',
      time: performance.now()
    };
  })
);
const stableLatest$ = zone.onStable
.pipe(
  map(() => {
    return {
      type: 'stable',
      time: performance.now()
    };
  })
);
```

The Performance API

 In this example, you'll use the performance API, a tool provided by the browser that can provide more precision than just Date.now(). As of this writing, it works on the latest version of all modern browsers and Internet Explorer. If you encounter any trouble using it, replace any calls to performance.now() with Date.now().

Next, we'll merge these two and add in the pairwise operator. pairwise is another operator that maintains internal state. On every event through the observable chain, pairwise emits both the newest event and the second-most-recent event. In this case, if the most-recent event is of type stable, we have all the information needed to determine how long the most-recent change detection cycle took. We don't want to use the combineLatest constructor you learned about in *Building Reactive Forms in Angular*, because that won't preserve the ordering, and we only want to take action if the latest event was stable. Now, we'll subscribe to this chain, logging the latest data to the console.

ng2/perf-complete/src/app/cd-profiler.service.ts
```
merge(
  unstableLatest$,
  stableLatest$
)
.pipe(
  pairwise(),
  filter(eventPair => eventPair[1].type === 'stable'),
  map(eventPair => eventPair[1].time - eventPair[0].time)
)
.subscribe((timing) => {
  console.log(`Change Detection took ${timing.toLocaleString()} ms`);
});
```

Finally, add this service to the constructor for the root module in app.module.ts (don't forget to import the service). Injecting it here is enough to get the service running, though it'll run in every environment. If you use a service like this for profiling your own apps, make sure that it doesn't run in prod.

ng2/perf-complete/src/app/app.module.ts
```
export class AppModule {
  constructor (private cd: CdProfilerService) {}
}
```

After this is all set up, reload the page. You should start seeing logs in the console detailing how long each change detection cycle took. Move a few patients around to trigger a few change detections. Note how long it took. Once you have details about the average length of a CD cycle, it's time to start making improvements.

The first CD is triggered when you click the "Change Ward" button. This only updates a CSS class and is satisfactorily quick. On the other hand, when someone changes the patient data through the ward dropdown, it takes ages.

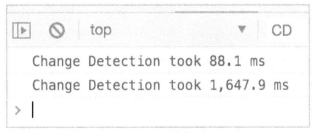

On a fairly modern computer, it takes almost two seconds to update a single patient. What's going on?

Optimizing Change Detection

Every change triggers a noticable pause in our hospital patient app. Angular is fast, but the app is currently forcing it to do thousands of checks anytime a change is made. Like with any performance issue, there are multiple solutions, but in this case, we'll focus on taking command of the change detection ourselves with the onPush strategy.

Each component comes with its own change detector, allowing us to selectively override how a component handles change detection. The onPush strategy relies on one or more observables annotated with @Input to do change detection. Instead of checking every round, components using onPush only run change detection when any of the annotated observables emit an event.

So what is this @Input annotation, anyway? Angular's tree structure means that information flows from the top (app.component.ts) down through the rest of the components. We can use @Input to explicitly determine what information we want to pass down the tree. @Input annotates a property of our component (the property can be of any type that's not a function).

Other Triggers for OnPush

While @Input is probably the most common way OnPush is triggered, A component using OnPush might run a change detection cycle two other ways: @Output and the async pipe. @Output works like @Input but pushes the data up the component tree through a parenthesis binding. As you know, the async pipe will create a subscription to the passed-in observable. When async is used in a component that uses OnPush, any events emitted by observables subscribed through async will also trigger change detection.

Let's open the row component that displays each row of patients. In the view (patient-row.component.html), you can see square brackets used to pass data about each patient to the patient-display component.

```
ng2/perf-complete/src/app/patient-row/patient-row.component.html
<div class="row">
  <app-patient-display
    class="col-xs-2"
    *ngFor="let patient of patientRowData"
    [patient]="patient"
  ></app-patient-display>
</div>
```

The row component iterates over all of the patients it has, passing the individual patient data into a component built to render patient data. Angular knows the patient attribute is what's used for the data, thanks to the following annotation in the patient component:

```
ng2/perf-complete/src/app/patient-display/patient-display.component.ts
export class PatientDisplayComponent implements OnInit {
  @Input() patient;
```

Without this annotation, Angular would not know to pass the data for the patient, and all the patient details components would be empty. However, @Input by itself does not optimize anything. It just says that some data can be passed through by some property. Next, let's import ChangeDetectionStrategy and update the patient component to use onPush.

```
ng2/perf-complete/src/app/patient-display/patient-display.component.ts
@Component({
  selector: 'app-patient-display',
  templateUrl: './patient-display.component.html',
  styleUrls: ['./patient-display.component.css'],
  changeDetection: ChangeDetectionStrategy.OnPush
})
```

This new strategy means that the component's change detector only runs when the value that's passed through by @Input changes. When the object in question is a regular, mutable object like it is currently, the change detector still needs to check the full equality of the object on every change detection cycle—a slow process. This is no way to increase performance. Instead, there are two options—make every patient object immutable (requires importing a third-party library) or use observables. When we annotate an observable with @Input, Angular handles it differently, treating every event in the observable stream as a "change" for the purpose of change detection. This allows us to precisely control when each cycle triggers, ensuring that no unneeded checks are run.

Joe asks:

Why Not Use OnPush in Every Component?

Using OnPush as a change detector means that change detection runs only when an @Input property changes. This means that the component has no ability to modify its own internal state. Components like the patient component that only display data and don't have any way to change their internal state are known as *presentational components*. A common application pattern is to have a parent container component that manages state and many presentational child components that merely handle rendering data to the page. This is why the Update Patient button is outside the patient display component.

For this to work, we need the row component to create an observable for the data of every patient. One way is to create an awkward method, using a BehaviorSubject so that the initial object is preserved for the component to subscribe to:

```
// in the row component
ngOnInit() {
  this.patientData = this.patientDataInput
    .map(this.createPatientObservable);
}

createPatientObservable(pData) {
  let patient$ = new BehaviorSubject();
  patient$.next(pData);

  return patient$;
}
```

With this new update, the row component now passes an observable through to the patient component. The patient component, with its new change detector, only checks to see what's new when that observable emits. It's a bit awkward to create the list of observables with the createPatientObservable method, and it requires a lot of rewiring throughout the application. If you're going to do a lot of rewiring anyway, it'd be better to switch to a tool suited to this problem: ngrx. ngrx is a tool you can use to control all of the state management in your application. This allows you to have more presentational components, further accelerating the application.

Managing State with ngrx

As you've just seen, handling state in an application can be tricky, especially when it comes time to optimize. In this section, you'll learn about ngrx, a tool you can use to model all of your application state as a series of observable streams. The application's state is centralized within ngrx, preventing rogue components from mistakenly modifying application state. This state centralization gives you precise control over how state can be modified by defining reducers. If you've ever used Redux, a lot of the same patterns apply.

Previously, applications would allow components to modify state without regard for the consequences. There was no concept of a "guard" in place to ensure that this centralized state could only be modified in approved ways. ngrx prescribes a set of patterns to bring order to this chaos. Specifically, a component emits a *dispatch event* when it wants to modify the application's state. ngrx has a *reducer function*, which handles how the dispatched event modifies the core state. Finally, the new state is broadcast to subscribers through RxJS.

> ### Joe asks:
> # That Sounds Really Complicated
>
> While that's not a question, it's a good point. State management tools like ngrx do require some forethought and setup. This extra work might not be worth it if you're just building a simple form page. On the other hand, plenty of big web applications need to change state from many different components, and ngrx fits quite nicely in that case. It's also important to remember that you don't need to put everything into your state management system—sometimes a value is only needed in a single component, and storing the state there is just fine.

Installing ngrx

The first step is to install the basic building blocks of ngrx with npm install @ngrx/core @nrgx/store. @nrgx/core is required to use any of the tools in the ngrx project. @ngrx/store is the tool you can use to define this central state object and the rules around modifying it. ngrx has many more utilities, and I encourage you to check them out, but they are outside the scope of this book.

Defining Actions

In ngrx parlance, an Action is a defined way that the application's state can be modified. In this case, the application has two different ways to modify the state: adding a list of patients (done in the initial load) and updating a single patient. Create a file (don't use the ng tool) named state.ts and add the following lines at the top:

```
ng2/perf-complete/src/app/state.ts
import { Action } from '@ngrx/store';

const ADD_PATIENTS = 'ADD_PATIENTS';
const UPDATE_PATIENT = 'UPDATE_PATIENT';

export class AddPatientsAction implements Action {
  type = ADD_PATIENTS;
  constructor(public payload) {}
}
export class UpdatePatientAction implements Action {
  type = UPDATE_PATIENT;
  constructor(public payload) {}
}

type PatientAction = AddPatientsAction | UpdatePatientAction;
```

Action types are defined as constant string. Nothing is stopping you from writing the string literal 'UPDATE_PATIENT' through the entire application—this would work the same as importing the declared action from state.ts. However, having a centralized declaration of action names prevents typos and makes the intent of the code much clearer.

Then, there are two classes—one for each type of action. These classes implement Action, which means that they conform to the definition of Action and can be used anywhere one would expect an Action. Specifically, they are passed into the reducers you define in the next section. Finally, a type keyword declares a PatientAction, which is a new type that can be either of the two actions defined above.

This is a lot of boilerplate for such a simple application. In larger, more complex apps, this typing data acts as a bumper guard, ensuring that code that modifies state (one of the most bug-prone areas of an application) stays true to its original intentions. Now that you've defined how this application's state can be modified, it's time to implement these actions in a reducer.

Creating Reducers

We need to define just how these state changes work. In state.ts, we'll define the patient reducer, a function that handles the UPDATE_PATIENT and ADD_PATIENTS actions. This application has only one type of state (an array of patients), but more complex apps have many different values stored in ngrx (user data, form elements, and the like).

ng2/perf-complete/src/app/state.ts

```
❶ export function patientReducer(state = [], action: PatientAction) {
❷   switch (action.type) {
      case UPDATE_PATIENT:
❸       return state.map((item, idx) =>
          idx === action.payload.index ? action.payload.newPatient : item
        );
❹     case ADD_PATIENTS:
        return [...state, ...action.payload];
❺     default:
        return state;
    }
  }
```

❶ Every reducer takes two parameters—the current state and the action to modify that state. It's good practice to include a default value for the state parameter, which becomes the initial application state. The action parameter might be undefined, when ngrx just wants to fetch the current state (this is why we have a default case in our switch statement). Otherwise, the action is defined as one of the two actions you defined in the previous section.

❷ Speaking of the switch statement, eventually this reducer needs to handle several different types of state change events. Reducers commonly include a switch statement to help organize all of the different goings-on that might occur with their slice of the overall state.

❸ Most importantly, we have the handler for the UPDATE_PATIENT event. In this case, it returns a new array of patients. This new array contains all the same patients as before, except for the one new patient containing the modified data from the event. The reducer returns a new array every time an action is dispatched with the UPDATE_PATIENT event. Every reducer should be a pure function, not modifying anything, but creating new arrays and objects when needed. Behind the scenes, ngrx uses object reference checks to determine what has changed. If our reducer modifies an object in place (and therefore, returns the same object reference when called), ngrx thinks nothing has changed and doesn't notify listeners. (A common mistake: Object.assign(currentState, { foo: "bar" }). This just updates currentState and does not create a new object.) Function purity also allows tools like @ngrx/store-devtools to keep track of state change history while you're debugging.

❹ Somehow we need to tell the reducer about all the patients in the ward. The service that fetches the patients could loop through a succession of dispatches of UPDATE_PATIENT, but this is much simpler. When the ADD_PATIENTS event is emitted, a new array containing both the old and new patients is returned.

❺ Every reducer should have a default case that returns the state as-is. This default is triggered in two cases: When the application is first initalized, ngrx calls all reducers without any parameters. In this case, the state parameter defaults to an empty array, and the switch returns the empty array as the initial state. The second case is when an action is dispatched to ngrx that this reducer doesn't handle. While this won't happen in this application, it's common to have many reducers that handle all kinds of actions.

Plugging It All Together

Now the reducer can handle two kinds of state changes. The next step is to update the application itself to talk to this new state store.

Updating the Root Module

Before you modify any components or services, you need to register ngrx and the reducer you created with the root module. Open app.module.ts and make the following modifications:

```
// Add imports
import { StoreModule } from '@ngrx/store';
import { patientReducer } from './state';

@NgModule({
  imports: [
    BrowserModule,
    ReactiveFormsModule,
    StoreModule.forRoot({
      patients: patientsReducer
    })
  ],
  ... etc
})
```

❶ forRoot sets up the store object you've just used throughout the rest of the application. The argument defines store—every key is a key of the store, as defined by the reducer passed in as the value.

In this case, a single property (patients) is set to whatever your reducer returns. Initially, this reducer will run with an empty action to create the initial state of an empty array.

Updating Existing Components

Currently, all state changes go through patient-data.service.ts. While that service still needs to generate the data (or in a real-world scenario, fetch it from a server), it should not be responsible for maintaining the state through the life cycle of the application. Instead, we need the components to listen directly to their slice of the store and dispatch events directly to that store when a change is requested.

Updating the Patient Service

First, make sure that the state is populated with data once it's been fetched. Components and services modify the state stored in ngrx by dispatching one of the actions you defined earlier. In this case, we want to dispatch the ADD_PATIENTS action and attach all of the patients generated in the service. The first thing to do is to import and inject the store service:

ng2/perf-complete/src/app/patient-data.service.ts
```
constructor(private store: Store<any>) {
```

The <any> part of the Store definition can be used to provide a type for the application state itself. In this case, any is provided because the state is not complicated. ngrx knows what to inject, thanks to the forRoot call in the application module. Now that the store is provided in the service, you need to dispatch an action. Import AddPatientsAction from state.ts and dispatch it:

```
ng2/perf-complete/src/app/patient-data.service.ts
this.store.dispatch(new AddPatientsAction(this.patients));
```

The store should be updated with the list of patients. Add a few log statements in patient-data.service.ts and state.ts until you're sure you understand what's happening. Once you're confident about how actions are dispatched, it's time to listen in to that data and display it on the page.

Listening in to Changes

At this point, ngrx initializes with an empty array and then populates with data generated by patient-data.service.ts. Next, the components need to listen in for changes to the state. Three components are involved here. Instead of reslicing state into rows each time, we can skip the row component and just use the display component, along with a few changes so that Bootstrap handles the rows for us. To allow this display, change the class on the root element in patient-display.component.html from row to col-xs-2. Update app.component.html to:

```
ng2/perf-complete/src/app/app.component.html
<app-patient-display
  *ngFor="let patient of patients$ | async"
  [patient]="patient"
></app-patient-display>
```

Now that the view code is out of the way, it's time to learn how to pull data out of the store. We can pluck a given slice out of the store by injecting it and calling the select method on our store. select returns an observable that triggers whenever the chosen slice of the state changes.

```
ng2/perf-complete/src/app/app.component.ts
ngOnInit() {
  this.patients$ = this.store.select('patients');
}
```

The Two Modes of select

The select method can act as two different operators. The first (and most common) uses treats select like pluck—takes in a string and delivers that slice of state. However, select can also be used as map, taking in a function that allows for more fine-grained control of the state slice delivered.

After you've entered all of this data, you'll notice a curious bug pop up: no data appears on the page. Now, one could argue that this means the application is more performant than ever, but that probably won't fly. The trouble here is a curious dependency resolution error. PatientDataService creates all of the patients, but only when it's injected. Currently, the service is only injected into the patientDisplay component. The patientDisplay component is only rendered when it has patients to display. To compensate, inject PatientDataService into app.component.ts.

@ngrx/effects

In the future, you could move PatientDataService to an effect from the @ngrx/effects library.

Sending Data to Store

The final step in converting your application to use ngrx is to update the patientDisplay component to dispatch an event to the service, much like you did when initializing the patient list. The same steps apply: inject the store with the Store<any> annotation and dispatch an event through the event constructor defined in state.ts, this time UpdatePatientAction.

`ng2/perf-complete/src/app/patient-display/patient-display.component.ts`
```
constructor(private patientData: PatientDataService,
            private store: Store<any>) { }

updateWard(newWard) {
  this.patient.currentWard = newWard;
  this.store.dispatch(new UpdatePatientAction(this.patient));
}
```

At this point, the application life cycle with ngrx has not functionally changed. However, the state of the application is gated and centralized. Anyone else who works on the application can clearly see the path a state change takes and know where and how to add new ways to modify state. It is much harder for the application to get into a bad state, since all interactions are clearly defined.

Additionally, you've fixed the massive performance bug; previously, reslicing the entire state into rows created a whole host of new arrays, bogging down performance. Now ngrx only recalculates when it absolutely needs to, speeding everything up.

As the application grows, keeping all of the actions and reducers in a single file might become a problem. When using ngrx in a production app, reducers are often kept in separate files along with their associated actions.

When ngrx Isn't Helpful

Using a state management tool like ngrx comes with a cost—even small updates to state can come with extensive boilerplate. It's probably overkill in this sample application. Even larger applications that mainly display data provided by a server might not have much to gain from ngrx. As with any major code change, make sure to do your research before you commit.

What We Learned

The things you learned in this chapter are certainly not basic tools. On the other hand, software developers don't work on basic applications. Each one is its own unique case, and I hope that the two techniques covered in this chapter will help you wrangle the difficult edge cases that reality inflicts upon our work. When your application starts slowing to a crawl, you can measure exactly what "a crawl" means. Once you've measured, it's time to break out observables and OnPush to optimize Angular's change detection passes.

On the other hand, you've also learned about ngrx and state mangement. Most software bugs are due to an application's state being set to something that was not intended (this is why "turn it off and on again" works—it resets the state). Rather than constantly asking users to refresh the page, you can now kill those bugs before they even spawn, taming the wild beast of state through reducers.

While Angular provides a solid, RxJS-powered backbone for framing your apps, you don't need Angular to use RxJS in a modern web application. In the next section of the book, you'll build out animations as well as a simple game using the canvas element. As part of the game, you'll build a small, RxJS-based framework of your own.

If you want to learn more about using RxJS for state management in an Angular application, here's a challenge for you. Above, the ngrx covered was creating, reading, and updating patient data. What we didn't cover was deleting. What needs to be done to add an event to remove a patient from the full list of patients?

CHAPTER 9

Reactive Game Development

Frontend development doesn't have to be dreary forms on repeat. It's always good to take a step back from the day-to-day and stretch yourself, especially if you learn new techniques along the way. In this chapter, you'll depart from typical webapp-based development and build a game using the <canvas> API defined by HTML5. As part of that, you'll learn about new Rx techniques to handle the rapid-fire state changes a game brings. Games also involve many moving objects, and you'll see how to use Rx's to create animations of all kinds. You'll also move beyond what the library provides and create your own operators. Long-time game developers and complete video game beginners will both learn something new from this chapter.

Using the Code Provided for this Section

 The code for this final chapter is provided in the canvas directory. Before you proceed, you need to run npm install. Run npm install to spin up a server that will serve your assets at http://localhost:8081. The code for the complete game is found in rxfighter-complete.

Creating Your Own Operator

So far, you've used operators provided by the RxJS library. However, you shouldn't be limited to those. With pipe, creating your own operators is easier than ever. An operator is a function that takes an observable, manipulates it in some way, and returns that new observable. This might be a bit complicated, so let's look at some code. In this simple case, an operator is created that appends a string to each value passed through the observable.

```
vanilla/canvasAnimation/operator-complete.ts
import { Observable } from 'rxjs';
import { map } from 'rxjs/operators';

❶ let stringAppendOperator = string => {
```

```
❷  return obs$ => {
     return obs$
     .pipe(map(val => val + string));
   };
 };
❸ let myObservable$ = new Observable(o => {
     o.next('hello');
     o.complete();
   });

   myObservable$.pipe(
     stringAppendOperator(' world!')
   )
   .subscribe(next => {
❹    console.log(next);
   });
```

❶ Each of the operators you've seen so far is a function that returns another function. In this case, the operator is a function that takes a string, so that the end developer can define what should be appended to each value—in this case, world!

❷ RxJS passes the observable to the inner function, and pipes it through the map operator to modify the value, appending the string.

❸ To test this, an observable is created that emits a single value, then completes.

❹ Finally, this should log 'hello world!'

This example cheats a bit by wrapping the map operator. Most operators included with RxJS create an entirely new observable, subscribe to the input observable, modifiy the value and return the newly-created observable. Here's how the map operator works:

```
let mapOperator = someMappingFunction => {
  return obs$ => {
    return new Observable(o => {
      let subscription = obs$.subscribe(
        val => o.next(someMappingFunction(val))
      );
      () => subscription.unsubscribe();
    });
  };
};
```

Creating a new observable gets pretty complicated, and is probably overkill for any operator you want to write, but it's good to have some understanding of what's happening behind the scenes whenever you call an operator.

All this seems like a very messy way to do what we already learned how to do: manipulate a stream using the operators Rx provides. However, the power of creating your own operators comes from the ability to create reusable, composable chunks of functionality.

Remember the stock streaming example from *Advanced Async?* Imagine we had multiple graphs on the page that all wanted to listen in on the stock filtering checkboxes. We could either copy and paste the same functionality for each graph, or create a single unit of functionality for that filtering and pass it into pipe:

```
function filterByCheckboxes(obs$) {
  return combineLatest(
    settings$,
    obs$,
    (enabledStocks, latestUpdates) => ({enabledStocks, latestUpdates})
  )
  .pipe(
    map(({enabledStocks, latestUpdates}) => {
      return latestUpdates
      .pipe(
        filter(stockHistory => enabledStocks.includes(stockHistory.name))
      );
    })
  );
}

stockPrices$
.pipe(filterByCheckboxes)
.subscribe(updatePricesGraph);

stockRatios$
.pipe(filterByCheckboxes)
.subscribe(updateRatiosGraph);

stockCaps$
.pipe(filterByCheckboxes)
.subscribe(updateCapsGraph);
```

So long as every stream ensures that the objects passed through have a name property that matches the stock ticker, this custom operator allows us to combine several operators together and reuse them across our applications. Now, what does this have to do with video games?

Animating Objects

The term *animation* covers a whole host of topics, but this section is concerned just with the subcategory of animation that details 'the process by which an object moves from point A to point B'. This type of animation is known as a 'tween' (since an object is moving be*tween* two points). The simplest possible tween consists of an element to move, the element's current location as a start point, an end point, and the amount of time the animation will take. Modeled in RxJS, it looks something like this:

vanilla/canvasAnimation/simpleTween-complete.ts
```
function simpleTween(element, endPoint, durationSec) {
  // Convert duration to 60 frames per second
  let durationInFrames = 60 * durationSec;
  let distancePerStep = endPoint / durationInFrames;

  // 60 frames per second
  interval(1000 / 60)
  .pipe(
    map(n => n * distancePerStep),
    take(durationInFrames)
  )
  .subscribe((location) => {
    element.style.left = location + 'px';
  });
}
```

As always, there's a catch. interval(1000 / 60) can only make a best effort attempt to emit at every interval—it provides no guarantee that it will emit an event *exactly* every 17 milliseconds. Every 17 milliseconds, RxJS asks the browser to execute a function. Many things could get in the way. If another function is currently being executed, our stream will be delayed. Browsers also throttle CPU usage of background tabs, so if the tab this is running in is not focused, the animation might get even further behind. Don't take my word for it—run the following code to see just how far behind this interval can get. After you've done that, refresh the page, then switch over to another tab. Switch back after a while, and things get even weirder:

vanilla/canvasAnimation/frames.ts
```
import { interval } from 'rxjs';
import { take, map, pairwise } from 'rxjs/operators';

interval(1000 / 60)
.pipe(
  take(60),
  map(() => performance.now()),
  pairwise(),
  map(lastTimestamps => lastTimestamps[1] - lastTimestamps[0]),
  map(msPerFrame => msPerFrame.toLocaleString())
)
.subscribe(msPerFrame =>
  console.log(`Last frame took ${msPerFrame}ms to run, ideally 17`)
);
```

On my relatively modern laptop, I got numbers ranging from 8.5 ms all the way up to 30 ms. Reload the tab, then switch away while the frame processing happens. The numbers get even worse! If a laptop can't keep an interval consistent, then there's no hope for users who are trying to watch our animations on a mobile phone. The lesson is that we can't count on "frames" as a unit of measurement if we want our animations to be timely. Instead, we need some measurement of how long it's been since the last time an event came down our stream. While it's possible to hack something together using performance.now() and pairwise like above, it's time to talk about the Rx tool we've been unknowingly using all this time: Schedulers.

Calling next with Schedulers

You've learned a heaping pile of different ways to create observables throughout this book. The secret you didn't know was how Rx decides exactly when to send a new value down the chain. The tool Rx uses for this is called a scheduler, and Rx ships many options for you to choose from. By default, every observable does not use a scheduler to plan out events, instead they emit all values synchronously. Run the following code to see this in action:

```
of('Hello')
.subscribe(next => console.log(next));

console.log('World');
```

This snippet does not pass a scheduler into the of constructor, so it just runs synchronously. This example logs Hello before World. Now, we can add the asap scheduler to the mix, which delays any events in the observable pipeline until all synchronous code is executed.

Behind the Scenes

 Specifically, the asap scheduler adds the next call to the microtask queue. This means that any observable using the asap scheduler behaves the same way as a promise.

```
of('Hello', Scheduler.asap)
.subscribe(next => console.log(next));

console.log('World');
```

When you run the updated code, you see World logged before Hello. The synchronous log at the end of the snippet runs, and then the observable, now running on an asynchronous schedule, emits an event, leading to World getting logged second. Most observable constructors take an optional scheduler as their final parameter. Several regular operators, like bufferTime, debounceTime, and delay also allow a user-defined scheduler.

Asynchronous schedulers

 RxJS has two different types of asynchronous schedulers: asap and async. The key difference is that asap schedules the observable event to be run using the micro task queue (process.nextTick() in Node.js, or setTimeout in the browser). This means that the event runs after any synchronous code but before any other scheduled asynchronous tasks. The other major scheduler, async, schedules using setTimeout, and is appropriate for some time-based operations.

Using an asynchronous scheduler is neat, but what's important for this chapter is the animationFrame scheduler, which runs every event through a call to the requestAnimationFrame API.

Requesting Repaints with requestAnimationFrame

In the world of the <canvas> API, we use requestAnimationFrame to inform the browser that we're going to write a batch of pixels to the page. This way, we can update the location of everything at once, and the browser only needs to repaint one time, as opposed to the browser redrawing the page for each object we want to write. It takes a single parameter, a function, that is typically called recursively. Most usage of requestAnimationFrame looks something like this:

```
function updateCanvas() {
  updateObjects();
  renderObjects();
  requestAnimationFrame(updateCanvas);
}
```

In our case, we don't need to muck around with manually calling requestAnimationFrame, we just need to set up our interval creation method with the proper scheduler. This results in more regular spacing between frame updates. The import is a bit wonky, so make sure you get it right:

```
import { animationFrame } from 'rxjs/internal/scheduler/animationFrame';

function rafTween(element, endPoint, durationSec) {
  // Convert duration to 60 frames per second
  let durationInFrames = 60 * durationSec;
  let distancePerStep = endPoint / durationInFrames;

  // 60 frames per second
  interval(1000 / 60, animationFrame)
  .pipe(
    map(n => n * distancePerStep),
    take(durationInFrames)
  )
```

```
  .subscribe((location) => {
    element.style.left = location + 'px';
  });
}
```

We're not quite there yet—blips in rendering time can still occur. Now that we added a scheduler to the mix, we have access to the now method on our scheduler. The now method works like the browser's performance.now, but it's integrated into the scheduler itself, keeping everything in one nice package. With one final update, we now have our tweening function ready for primetime. It will try to run at sixty frames per second, but will be able to handle a slower machine without problems by expanding how far the object moves each frame:

vanilla/canvasAnimation/rafTween-complete.ts
```
function rafTween(element, pixelsToMove, durationSec) {
  let startTime = animationFrame.now();
  let endTime = animationFrame.now() + (durationSec * 1000);
  let durationMs = endTime - startTime;
  let startPoint = element.style.left;

  interval(1000 / 60, animationFrame)
  .pipe(
    map(() => (animationFrame.now() - startTime) / durationMs),
    takeWhile(percentDone => percentDone <= 1)
  )
  .subscribe(percentDone => {
    element.style.left = startPoint + (pixelsToMove * percentDone) + 'px';
  });
}
```

❶ The first thing we do is ignore the value emitted from interval and instead, map the time elapsed since start as a percentage of total time the animation will take.

❷ Now that we no longer can depend on a number of events (frames) to determine when we're done, we add the takeWhile operator, which continues to pass events through until duration milliseconds have passed. Since it gets a value representing the percentage completion of the animation, we're done when that percentage reaches 1.

Creating Easing Operators

Now that the observable stream emits progressive values, we can run them through a converter to create different styles of transitioning between two points (also known as easing). Each possible easing relies on an equation that answers the question, "Given that we are halfway through, where should the center be rendered?" For instance, the following starts slowly, and then accelerates to catch up at the end:

```
function easingSquared(percentDone) {
  return percentDone * percentDone;
}

easingSquared(.25) // 0.0625
easingSquared(.50) // 0.25
easingSquared(.75) // 0.5625
easingSquared(.9) // 0.81
easingSquared(1) // 1
```

Many other easing functions exist, but it's a lot more fun to see them in action than to drearily read code.

Let's put everything together from this section to create a tool that allows moving elements with an arbitrary easing function to see a few of these in action. Open multiTween.ts and write the following code.

First, we'll create a percentDone operator that takes a duration in milliseconds and returns a percentage of how far the animation has gone.

```
vanilla/canvasAnimation/multiTween-complete.ts
function percentDone(durationSec) {
  return function ($obs) {
    let startTime = animationFrame.now();
    // let endTime = animationFrame.now() + (durationSec * 1000);
    // let durationMs = endTime - startTime;
    return $obs.pipe(
      map(() => (animationFrame.now() - startTime) / (durationSec * 1000))
    );
  };
}
```

While this function creates a startTime variable, rest assured that the inner function won't be called until something subscribes to the observable—another advantage of lazy observables. This means that startTime won't be set until the animation begins.

The next operator uses a map that takes an easing function. Right now, this is just a wrapper around the map operator.

```
vanilla/canvasAnimation/multiTween-complete.ts
function easingMap(easingFn) {
  return function ($obs) {
    return $obs.pipe(map(easingFn));
  };
}
```

This snippet may seem superfluous (why not just use map?), but it helps communicate intent. Later, you can add more concrete types to your operator with TypeScript, so that it will allow only certain types of functions.

Finally, let's create a new tween function that takes advantage of these two new operators you created.

vanilla/canvasAnimation/multiTween-complete.ts
```
function finalTween(easingFn, element, endPoint, duration) {
  let startPoint = element.style.left;
  let pixelsToMove = endPoint - startPoint;

  interval(1000 / 60, animationFrame)
  .pipe(
    percentDone(duration),
    takeWhile(percentDone => percentDone <= 1),
    easingMap(easingFn)
  )
  .subscribe((movePercent: number) => {
    element.style.left = startPoint + (pixelsToMove * movePercent) + 'px';
  });
}
```

We can then compose these together to demonstrate what several different types of easing operators look like:

vanilla/canvasAnimation/multiTween-complete.ts
```
// Easing Functions
let linear = p => p;
let quadraticIn = p => p * p;
let quadraticOut = p => p * (2 - p);

finalTween(linear, redSquare, 500, 5);
finalTween(quadraticIn, blueSquare, 500, 5);
finalTween(quadraticOut, greenSquare, 500, 5);
```

Architecting a Game

Now let's move beyond simple animations and start adding interactivity. In this section, you'll put together an entire game using RxJS. I've already built out just enough for you to start plugging things together with observables. Don't hesitate to read through these prebuilt sections, but understanding them is not required for the neat, new RxJS tricks you'll learn through the rest of the chapter.

Before anything else, let's talk about why you'd want to use RxJS in such a game. The skeleton of this project has been created for you in rxfighter, with the complete project available to read in rxfighter-complete. As always, I recommend that you build your own project before you peek into the code for the completed one. We can totally take a peek at what the finished project should look like—it's important to know what you're going for.

RxFighter

Drawing to a Canvas Element

The HTML5 standard introduced the <canvas> element as a way to more easily create interactive experiences in the browser. It was designed as a native replacement for Flash, avoiding the many security issues present while staying right in the core of the browser. Canvas exposes a set of APIs that allow you to programmatically draw to the page.

canvas/rxfighter-complete/index.ts
```
let canvas = <HTMLCanvasElement>document.querySelector('canvas');
❶ export let ctx = canvas.getContext('2d');
❷ canvas.width = config.canvas.width;
canvas.height = config.canvas.height;
```

❶ The first thing to do is to grab the canvas element off of the page and get the context from it. The context object is the tool we'll use to interact with the page.

❷ There's a quirk in canvas where the height and width of the element can be out of sync with the values stored on the JavaScript side, leading to odd stretching or compression of the values you write to the page. With that in mind, it's important to sync those values right at the start to avoid errors.

Now everything's set up and you can use the ctx to start drawing things to the canvas. Everything drawn to a canvas stays there until something else is drawn over it. You can't have old frames lingering around, so the first thing to write up is a function that clears the canvas by drawing over the entire thing.

```
canvas/rxfighter-complete/index.ts
function clearCanvas() {
  ctx.fillStyle = '#000';
  ctx.fillRect(0, 0, canvas.width, canvas.height);
}
```

There are two steps here. First, we tell the context we want the fill to be black (you can set it using hex or RGB, just like CSS). Secondly, we tell it to draw a rectangle, starting at 0, 0 (the upper left coordinate) and extend the entire size of the canvas. Add a call to clearCanvas and you should see a black square appear on the page. First step down! Now, on to interactivity and animations.

The RxJS Backbone

For a game to work, every frame, we need to go through every item in the game, make any changes to the item's state, and then render everything on the page. RxJS lets us declaratively state each step through custom operators and tap. Our custom operators take in the entire observable, so each item has the complete freedom to do whatever it needs to along the way through the entire RxJS API. Once the updates are done, tap lets us call the render functions safely, ensuring that errant code won't accidentally update the state. Open index.ts and fill in the following, importing as needed:

```
let gameState = new GameState();

interval(17, animationFrame)
.pipe(
  mapTo(gameState),
  tap(clearCanvas)
)
.subscribe((newGameState: GameState) => {
  Object.assign(gameState, newGameState);
});
```

This backbone starts off by creating a new instance of the game state. The game loop is created using interval and the animationFrame scheduler you learned about earlier. The first operator, mapTo throws away the interval's increasing integer and passes on the current state to the rest of the observable chain. The mapTo is followed by a tap call to the canvas-clearing function you wrote earlier. Finally, a subscription kicks off the next cycle, saving the new game state for the next frame.

> ### Joe asks:
> ## Why Use Object.assign Instead of Just Assigning?
>
> There's a little quirk here with mapTo. It takes a variable, ignores any input, and passes on the passed-in variable. More importantly, it takes a reference to that variable. If the subscribe ran gameState = newGameState;, then gameState would contain the new state, but the old reference (which is what mapTo is looking at) would contain stale data. Instead, this uses Object.assign to update the old reference with new data.

The rest of this game follows a pattern for each item (or collection of items). Each file exports two functions: a custom operator that takes the game state and manipulates the objects contained therein. The second is passed in to tap and contains the logic for rendering those objects to the page.

This backbone also allows us to easily see and change the order things are rendered in. Canvas being a "last write wins" world, it's key to ensure that the background is drawn before the player. Now that the backbone has been established, it's time to talk about how to manage state manipulation through the lifetime of this game.

Managing Game State

Keeping a game's state in sync with the variety of different events that can happen at any point in the game is quite the challenge. Add the requirement that it all needs to render smoothly at sixty frames per second, and life gets very difficult. Let's take a few lessons from the ngrx section in *Advanced Angular* and add in a canvas flavor to ensure a consistent gameplay experience.

First, open gameState.ts and take a look at the initial game state. We're using a class so that resetting the game state is as easy as new GameState(). Like ngrx, this is a centralized state object that represents the state of everything in the game. Unlike ngrx, we'll ditch the reducers and instead rely on pure RxJS as the backbone of our state management. We'll do this by splitting the game into individual units of content (the player, background, enemy) and centralizing each unit of content into two parts: the update step and the render step. Let's start with something simple—the background.

Shooting Stars

The background consists of 100 stars of various sizes moving around at different paces. The star object itself contains its current location, as well as its velocity. Open up stars.ts and you see two functions: updateStars and renderStars. Both of these functions are called once per frame. updateStars is passed into the first half of the backbone, with renderStars passed into the tap operator in the second half.

Each star needs to move down the canvas every frame. With our system, that means updating the x coordinate of the star. If the star has moved past the bottom of the screen, we reposition it to a random point back at the top of the screen:

canvas/rxfighter-complete/stars.ts
```
export function updateStars(gameState$: Observable<GameState>) {
  return gameState$
  .pipe(
    map(state => {
      state.stars.forEach(star => {
        star.y += star.dy;
        if (star.y > config.canvas.height) {
          star.x = randInt(0, config.canvas.width);
          star.y = 0;
        }
      });
      return state;
    })
  );
}
```

On Pure Functions

Part of knowing best practices is knowing when to break them. Technically, these functions that update the game state should create a new object every time we manipulate state to ensure each function is pure. However, creating new objects and arrays in JavaScript is expensive. If we want to push 60 frames per section, that means that we only have 16.7 milliseconds to update each frame. As a compromise, we reuse the same object, but keep state changes isolated as much as possible. This also means we avoid using array methods, such as map and filter, as they create a new array behind the scenes.

The render function also makes the same loop over the stars array, this time writing pixels to the canvas. fillStyle, which you saw before, is set to white, and then each star is drawn to its location:

canvas/rxfighter-complete/stars.ts
```
export function renderStars(state: GameState) {
  ctx.fillStyle = '#fff';
  state.stars.forEach(star => {
    ctx.fillRect(star.x, star.y, star.size, star.size);
  });
}
```

Joe asks:

Why don't we just combine these into a single function?

While I'm always in favor of not doing two things when one thing suffices, separating the update from the render has two key advantages. First, the render and update code serve very different purposes. I'm a stickler about keeping state changes isolated whenever possible. Any state change has a single place, which saves time when debugging. Secondly, this allows us to control the ordering of update and rendering events independently of each other, allowing for a more flexible program.

Tracking User Input

Tracking and updating the stars was fairly simple—every frame required the same update. Let's try something more challenging. Our game needs a player, otherwise it'll be pretty boring. Instead of the same update every time, our player update function needs to figure out what keys are currently being pressed and move the player's ship around. First, we need to track keyboard state. Open gameState.ts and add the following:

```
canvas/rxfighter-complete/gameState.ts
// Keep track of the state of all movement keys
let keyStatus = {};
fromEvent(document, 'keydown')
.subscribe((e: any) => {
  keyStatus[e.keyCode] = true;
});

fromEvent(document, 'keyup')
.subscribe((e: any) => {
  keyStatus[e.keyCode] = false;
});
```

This keyStatus object tracks the state of the entire keyboard. We create it outside of the GameState class, so that it only needs to be initialized once. Now that we know what keys the player is pressing, it's time to update the state. Open player.ts and start filling it out with the following:

```
canvas/rxfighter-complete/player.ts
function updatePlayerState(gameState: GameState): GameState {
  if (gameState.keyStatus[config.controls.left]) {
    gameState.player.x -= config.ship.speed;
  }
  if (gameState.keyStatus[config.controls.right]) {
    gameState.player.x += config.ship.speed;
  }
```

> \//   **Joe asks:**
> ’ᵕ’   # What if the player releases the key halfway through our update step?
>
> The update and render steps still execute as one synchronous unit. There is a gap between them for any other updates to happen. If the user releases the spacebar, the browser makes a note to send an event down the keyup observable chain whenever the event loop clears up. This means that when the update/render steps start executing, we can be sure that the key state stays the same throughout.

```
if (gameState.player.x < 0) {
  gameState.player.x = 0;
}
if (gameState.player.x > (config.canvas.width - config.ship.width)) {
  gameState.player.x = (config.canvas.width - config.ship.width);
}
return gameState;
}
```

So far this is pretty simple—if the left key is pressed, move left; if the right key is pressed, move right. If both keys are pressed, move the player to the left and then back to center again. This is slightly inefficient, but harmless in the grand scheme of things. Following that are two checks to make sure the player doesn't slide off the edge of the screen. Now that the player can move about, let's make sure they can see the results of their actions. Fill out renderPlayer with a simple image display (but only if they haven't been hit yet):

canvas/rxfighter-complete/player.ts
```
export function renderPlayer(state: GameState) {
  if (!state.player.alive) { return; }
  ctx.drawImage(playerImg, state.player.x, state.player.y);
}
```

You'll notice that updatePlayerStatus isn't exported. That's because there's a bit more to do in this file. You need to write a third function, updatePlayer, in player.ts, that just takes an observable stream and maps it past the updatePlayerStatus function we just wrote. This is the actual operator that this file will export.

```
export const updatePlayer = (obs: Observable<GameState>) => {
  return obs
  .pipe(
    map(updatePlayerState)
  );
};
```

You'll see why this function is separate in the next section. For now, import updatePlayer and renderPlayer into index.ts and add them to the observable backbone. At this point, you should see your ship flying across a starfield and be able to move left and right. Unfortunately, this tranquil spaceflight is about to be interrupted by some aggressive Space Pirates! We need to equip our player with some weapons before they become a rapidly-expanding cloud of vapor.

Building a Complex Operator

Now it's time to put on our game designer hats and figure out what sort of weapons we should give the player. If we give the player a laser cannon that can fire on every frame, then they're practically invulnerable. That's no fun at all. We'll need to limit how often the player's laser can fire. We'll need an observable operator that can take the game state, check to see whether a given condition is true (spacebar is pressed) and whether a given amount of time has passed since the last time it fired. Alas, RxJS doesn't have this built in—but it does contain the tools for us to build such an operator ourselves. Open util.ts and add the following function:

```
canvas/rxfighter-complete/util.ts
export function triggerEvery(
  mapper,
  timeInterval: () => number,
  condition?: (gameState$: GameState) => boolean
) {
  let nextValidTrigger;
  return function (obs$: Observable<GameState>) {
    return obs$.pipe(map((gameState: GameState): GameState => {
      if (condition && !condition(gameState)) {
        return gameState;
      }
      if (nextValidTrigger > performance.now()) {
        return gameState;
      }
      nextValidTrigger = performance.now() + timeInterval();
      return mapper(gameState);
    }));
  };
}
```

You'll notice that you've just written another operator! The outer function allows us to customize how and when the lasers fire, while the inner encapsulates the logic and tracks how long it's been since the last fire. Let's write some values for the three methods this requires. Open player.ts and add this code:

canvas/rxfighter-complete/player.ts
```
let playerFire = (gameState: GameState) => {
  let availableLaser = gameState.player.lasers.find(l => l.y
                       - config.laser.height < 0);
  if (!availableLaser) { return gameState; }
  availableLaser.x = gameState.player.x + (config.ship.width / 2)
                     - (config.laser.width / 2);
  availableLaser.y = gameState.player.y;
  return gameState;
};
let fiveHundredMs = () => 500;
let isSpacebar = (gameState: GameState) =>
                 gameState.keyStatus[config.controls.fireLaser];
```

playerFire is our runIfTrue. It finds a laser attached to the player object that isn't currently on screen (remember, we're reusing objects instead of constantly creating new ones). If it finds an available laser object, it sets the laser's position to just in front of the player's current position. fivehundredms simply returns the number 500. This function will get more exciting when the space pirates come into play. Finally, we have a filtering function that checks to ensure the spacebar is currently pressed.

We're almost there—the lasers will appear, but nothing's in charge of updating them. Add a function to handle the laser state updating:

canvas/rxfighter-complete/player.ts
```
function updatePlayerLasers(gameState: GameState): GameState {
  // Lasers actually move
  gameState.player.lasers
    .forEach(l => {
      l.y -= config.laser.speed;
    });
  return gameState;
}
```

Now we need to add the firing and updating of the player's lasers to the updatePlayer method:

canvas/rxfighter-complete/player.ts
```
export const updatePlayer = (obs: Observable<GameState>) => {
  return obs
  .pipe(
    map(updatePlayerState),
    map(updatePlayerLasers),
    triggerEvery(playerFire, fiveHundredMs, isSpacebar)
  );
};
```

Add a new render function in lasers.ts and import the function into the backbone in index.ts:

```
canvas/rxfighter-complete/lasers.ts
export function renderLasers(state: GameState) {
  state.player.lasers
    .filter(l => l.y + config.laser.height > 0)
    .forEach(laser => {
      ctx.fillStyle = '#6f4';
      ctx.fillRect(laser.x, laser.y, config.laser.width, config.laser.height);
    });
  state.enemy.lasers
    .filter(l => l.y + config.laser.height > 0)
    .forEach(laser => {
      ctx.fillStyle = '#f64';
      ctx.fillRect(laser.x, laser.y, config.laser.width, config.laser.height);
    });
}
```

Now the player can dodge left and right while simultaneously firing their laser. Time to bring out the space pirates.

Creating Enemies

The space pirates are vicious, diving in and firing randomly. Our player needs to be alert and quick to survive. The programming for the enemy needs to handle spawning, flying about, and firing. We can borrow some concepts from player.ts, but most of them will require new code. Open up enemy.ts and create a new function updateEnemyState with the same signature as updatePlayerState. The first thing in this function is to determine whether we should spawn a new enemy ship:

```
canvas/rxfighter-complete/enemy.ts
// Enemy appears, moves down 1/3 of the map, then turns
// Spawn a new enemy ship if needed
if (gameState.enemy.x <= -config.enemy.width ||
  gameState.enemy.x > config.canvas.width ||
  !gameState.enemy.alive
) {
  let xStart = randInt(
    config.enemy.width,
    config.canvas.width - config.enemy.width
  );
  gameState.enemy.alive = true;
  gameState.enemy.y = -config.enemy.height;
  gameState.enemy.x = xStart;
  gameState.enemy.dy = config.enemy.speed;
  gameState.enemy.dx = 0;
}
```

If the enemy has moved offscreen, or they've been hit by the player, we should create a new enemy just off the upper edge of the screen. This one's alive and coming for revenge. The dy property is initially set, causing the pirate to move downward along the y axis. There's no lateral movement in the first phase, so dx is set to 0.

Joe asks:

What does the d stand for?

The d in dx/dy stands for "change". It comes from the mathematical symbol delta, which indicates a change in something. In most canvas contexts, it's a convention used to represent "this object is moving along an axis at this speed."

Now that the enemy has spawned, it's time to move them toward the player. The enemy ship should move down the top third of the screen, then turn to a side and escape.

```
canvas/rxfighter-complete/enemy.ts
// Once 1/3 point is reached, turn to a side
if (gameState.enemy.y >= config.canvas.height / 3 &&
  gameState.enemy.dx === 0
) {
  let leftOrRight = Math.random() > 0.5;
  gameState.enemy.dy = 0;
  gameState.enemy.dx = config.enemy.speed * (leftOrRight ? 1 : -1);
}
```

Finally, we need to update the x/y coordinates of the enemy ship; otherwise it'll just hang offscreen for eternity:

```
canvas/rxfighter-complete/enemy.ts
gameState.enemy.x += gameState.enemy.dx;
gameState.enemy.y += gameState.enemy.dy;
return gameState;
```

You'll also want to add a function to update the lasers property on the enemy. This works the same way as the lasers from the player's ship.

```
canvas/rxfighter-complete/enemy.ts
function updateEnemyLasers(gameState: GameState): GameState {
  gameState.enemy.lasers
    .forEach(l => l.y += config.laser.speed);
  return gameState;
}
```

Enemy laser firing presents a different design problem. We're less worried about the current state of the keyboard and more about creating an engaging challenge. We can reuse triggerEvery, but need to pass in a new set of criteria. We'll skip the condition parameter—whenever the pirates have an opportunity to fire, they will. Instead, we create a random time interval and fire a laser whenever that time is up:

```
canvas/rxfighter-complete/enemy.ts
let nextEnemyFire = () => randInt(500, 1500);
function fireEnemyLaser(gameState: GameState): GameState {
  let availableLaser = gameState.enemy.lasers.find(l =>
    l.y > config.canvas.height + config.laser.height
  );
  if (!availableLaser) { return gameState; }
  let offset = (config.enemy.width / 2) - (config.laser.width / 2);
  availableLaser.x = gameState.enemy.x + offset;
  availableLaser.y = gameState.enemy.y + config.enemy.height;
  return gameState;
}
```

Now that all this state manipulation is set up, we'll attach it to the Rx backbone with the same update/render pattern as the player ship:

```
canvas/rxfighter-complete/enemy.ts
export function updateEnemies(obs: Observable<GameState>) {
  return obs
  .pipe(
    map(updateEnemyState),
    map(updateEnemyLasers),
    triggerEvery(fireEnemyLaser, nextEnemyFire)
  );
}

export function renderEnemies(state: GameState) {
  ctx.drawImage(enemyImg, state.enemy.x, state.enemy.y);
}
```

Now we've got a rousing space battle on our hands—player and pirate fighting back and forth in a desperate battle for survival! Except both will easily survive—we haven't programmed in any sort of collision detection or destruction mechanics. Time to fix that.

Detecting Collisions

This game won't be any fun if there's no element of danger. Open up collisions.ts and take a look around. I've filled in the math stuff that isn't as relevant to the Rx core. There's a checkCollision function that operates much like the other updates you've seen. This one's filled out, since it's more of the same that you've already written. One thing that sticks out is a tracker for how many frames have elapsed since an explosion happened.

```
gameState.explosions.forEach(e =>
  e.framesSince++;
);
```

We need to track this value since the explosion is animated. Canvas doesn't allow traditional gifs, so we need to manually animate. Let's skip ahead to the render function and see how that plays out:

canvas/rxfighter-complete/collisions.ts
```
export function renderExplosions (gameState: GameState) {
  gameState.explosions.forEach(e => {
    if (e.framesSince > config.explosion.frames *
          config.explosion.gameFramesPer) { return; }
    ctx.drawImage(
      explosionImg,
      Math.floor(e.framesSince / config.explosion.gameFramesPer) *
                config.explosion.width,
      0,
      config.explosion.width,
      config.explosion.height,
      e.x,
      e.y,
      config[e.type].width,
      config[e.type].height
    );
  });
}
```

This function iterates over all of the explosions attached to the game state, skipping over the ones that completed their animation. If an explosion is still animating, we draw an image (just like the player/pirate ships), but instead of a static image, we draw a single frame from a sprite sheet. This sprite sheet is a single image that contains every frame of the animation. Instead of drawing the entire image, we draw only a subsection.

Add checkCollision and renderExplosions to the Rx backbone in index.ts. At this point, you have a colliding function, a type definition for explosion, and two sets of lasers to check. Try to figure out what you need to write inside checkCollision to get the game to update. Hint: don't forget to set alive to false. If you get stuck, don't worry; take a peek at the answer in the rxfighter-finished folder.

What We Learned

At this point, you've got a perfectly functioning, if simple, browser-based spaceship game. Along the way, you learned about the power of creating your own operators and how they can not only be used to create new observables, but pass around the root observable chain, allowing you to isolate changes. You also picked up some animation techniques that work in both the canvas world and the regular DOM. Speaking of canvas, you learned the basic APIs and can now start venturing into building all sorts of games.

Bonus Points

The sky's not the limit—you're already in space! There's plenty more you can do with this game. First, death shouldn't be permanent. Add a restart functionality (but don't forget to prevent restart if the player's still alive). You could also add in a point system—how many space pirates can the player take out before the player's eventual demise? Perhaps the space pirates have more in store for our adventurous player—new weapons, new ships, new powerups. These new ships could use the easing patterns from the animation section to create more challenging flight paths. If you're feeling particularly energized after finishing this chapter, you might want to look into server-side RxJS and build a multiplayer game for all your friends to enjoy.

If you're interested in learning more about HTML5 and canvas, you can check out Brian Hogan's book on the topic,[1] also from The Pragmatic Bookshelf.

---

1. https://pragprog.com/book/bhh52e/html5-and-css3

Index

Thank you!

How did you enjoy this book? Please let us know. Take a moment and email us at support@pragprog.com with your feedback. Tell us your story and you could win free ebooks. Please use the subject line "Book Feedback."

Ready for your next great Pragmatic Bookshelf book? Come on over to https://pragprog.com and use the coupon code BUYANOTHER2019 to save 30% on your next ebook.

Void where prohibited, restricted, or otherwise unwelcome. Do not use ebooks near water. If rash persists, see a doctor. Doesn't apply to *The Pragmatic Programmer* ebook because it's older than The Pragmatic Bookshelf itself. Side effects may include increased knowledge and skill, increased marketability, and deep satisfaction. Increase dosage regularly.

And thank you for your continued support,

Andy Hunt, Publisher

SAVE 30%!
Use coupon code
BUYANOTHER2019

JavaScript and more JavaScript

JavaScript is back and better than ever. Rediscover the latest features and best practices for this ubiquitous language.

Rediscovering JavaScript

JavaScript is no longer to be feared or loathed—the world's most popular and ubiquitous language has evolved into a respectable language. Whether you're writing frontend applications or server-side code, the phenomenal features from ES6 and beyond—like the rest operator, generators, destructuring, object literals, arrow functions, modern classes, promises, async, and metaprogramming capabilities—will get you excited and eager to program with JavaScript. You've found the right book to get started quickly and dive deep into the essence of modern JavaScript. Learn practical tips to apply the elegant parts of the language and the gotchas to avoid.

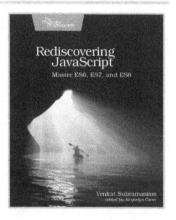

Venkat Subramaniam
(286 pages) ISBN: 9781680505467. $45.95
https://pragprog.com/book/ves6

Simplifying JavaScript

The best modern JavaScript is simple, readable, and predictable. Learn to write modern JavaScript not by memorizing a list of new syntax, but with practical examples of how syntax changes can make code more expressive. Starting from variable declarations that communicate intention clearly, see how modern principles can improve all parts of code. Incorporate ideas with curried functions, array methods, classes, and more to create code that does more with less while yielding fewer bugs.

Joe Morgan
(282 pages) ISBN: 9781680502886. $47.95
https://pragprog.com/book/es6tips

Better by Design

From architecture and design to deployment in the harsh realities of the real world, make your software better by design.

Design It!

Don't engineer by coincidence—design it like you mean it! Grounded by fundamentals and filled with practical design methods, this is the perfect introduction to software architecture for programmers who are ready to grow their design skills. Ask the right stakeholders the right questions, explore design options, share your design decisions, and facilitate collaborative workshops that are fast, effective, and fun. Become a better programmer, leader, and designer. Use your new skills to lead your team in implementing software with the right capabilities—and develop awesome software!

Michael Keeling
(358 pages) ISBN: 9781680502091. $41.95
https://pragprog.com/book/mkdsa

Release It! Second Edition

A single dramatic software failure can cost a company millions of dollars—but can be avoided with simple changes to design and architecture. This new edition of the best-selling industry standard shows you how to create systems that run longer, with fewer failures, and recover better when bad things happen. New coverage includes DevOps, microservices, and cloud-native architecture. Stability antipatterns have grown to include systemic problems in large-scale systems. This is a must-have pragmatic guide to engineering for production systems.

Michael Nygard
(376 pages) ISBN: 9781680502398. $47.95
https://pragprog.com/book/mnee2

The Modern Web

Get up to speed on the latest HTML, CSS, and JavaScript techniques, and secure your Node applications.

HTML5 and CSS3 (2nd edition)

HTML5 and CSS3 are more than just buzzwords – they're the foundation for today's web applications. This book gets you up to speed on the HTML5 elements and CSS3 features you can use right now in your current projects, with backwards compatible solutions that ensure that you don't leave users of older browsers behind. This new edition covers even more new features, including CSS animations, IndexedDB, and client-side validations.

Brian P. Hogan
(314 pages) ISBN: 9781937785598. $38
https://pragprog.com/book/bhh52e

Secure Your Node.js Web Application

Cyber-criminals have your web applications in their crosshairs. They search for and exploit common security mistakes in your web application to steal user data. Learn how you can secure your Node.js applications, database and web server to avoid these security holes. Discover the primary attack vectors against web applications, and implement security best practices and effective countermeasures. Coding securely will make you a stronger web developer and analyst, and you'll protect your users.

Karl Düüna
(230 pages) ISBN: 9781680500851. $36
https://pragprog.com/book/kdnodesec

Long Live the Command Line!

Use tmux and Vim for incredible mouse-free productivity.

tmux 2

Your mouse is slowing you down. The time you spend
context switching between your editor and your con-
soles eats away at your productivity. Take control of
your environment with tmux, a terminal multiplexer
that you can tailor to your workflow. With this updated
second edition for tmux 2.3, you'll customize, script,
and leverage tmux's unique abilities to craft a produc-
tive terminal environment that lets you keep your fin-
gers on your keyboard's home row.

Brian P. Hogan
(102 pages) ISBN: 9781680502213. $21.95
https://pragprog.com/book/bhtmux2

Modern Vim

Turn Vim into a full-blown development environment
using Vim 8's new features and this sequel to the
beloved bestseller *Practical Vim*. Integrate your editor
with tools for building, testing, linting, indexing, and
searching your codebase. Discover the future of Vim
with Neovim: a fork of Vim that includes a built-in
terminal emulator that will transform your workflow.
Whether you choose to switch to Neovim or stick with
Vim 8, you'll be a better developer.

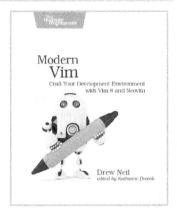

Drew Neil
(166 pages) ISBN: 9781680502626. $39.95
https://pragprog.com/book/modvim

The Joy of Mazes and Math

Rediscover the joy and fascinating weirdness of mazes and pure mathematics.

Mazes for Programmers

A book on mazes? Seriously?

Yes!

Not because you spend your day creating mazes, or because you particularly like solving mazes.

But because it's fun. Remember when programming used to be fun? This book takes you back to those days when you were starting to program, and you wanted to make your code do things, draw things, and solve puzzles. It's fun because it lets you explore and grow your code, and reminds you how it feels to just think.

Sometimes it feels like you live your life in a maze of twisty little passages, all alike. Now you can code your way out.

Jamis Buck
(286 pages) ISBN: 9781680500554. $38
https://pragprog.com/book/jbmaze

Good Math

Mathematics is beautiful—and it can be fun and exciting as well as practical. *Good Math* is your guide to some of the most intriguing topics from two thousand years of mathematics: from Egyptian fractions to Turing machines; from the real meaning of numbers to proof trees, group symmetry, and mechanical computation. If you've ever wondered what lay beyond the proofs you struggled to complete in high school geometry, or what limits the capabilities of the computer on your desk, this is the book for you.

Mark C. Chu-Carroll
(282 pages) ISBN: 9781937785338. $34
https://pragprog.com/book/mcmath

The Pragmatic Bookshelf

The Pragmatic Bookshelf features books written by developers for developers. The titles continue the well-known Pragmatic Programmer style and continue to garner awards and rave reviews. As development gets more and more difficult, the Pragmatic Programmers will be there with more titles and products to help you stay on top of your game.

Visit Us Online

This Book's Home Page
https://pragprog.com/book/rkrxjs
Source code from this book, errata, and other resources. Come give us feedback, too!

Keep Up to Date
https://pragprog.com
Join our announcement mailing list (low volume) or follow us on twitter @pragprog for new titles, sales, coupons, hot tips, and more.

New and Noteworthy
https://pragprog.com/news
Check out the latest pragmatic developments, new titles and other offerings.

Save on the eBook

Save on the eBook versions of this title. Owning the paper version of this book entitles you to purchase the electronic versions at a terrific discount.

PDFs are great for carrying around on your laptop—they are hyperlinked, have color, and are fully searchable. Most titles are also available for the iPhone and iPod touch, Amazon Kindle, and other popular e-book readers.

Buy now at *https://pragprog.com/coupon*

Contact Us

Online Orders:	*https://pragprog.com/catalog*
Customer Service:	*support@pragprog.com*
International Rights:	*translations@pragprog.com*
Academic Use:	*academic@pragprog.com*
Write for Us:	*http://write-for-us.pragprog.com*
Or Call:	+1 800-699-7764

CPSIA information can be obtained
at www.ICGtesting.com
Printed in the USA
JSHW031246020821
17473JS00006B/207